C000213379

James Bunting is a perform
recently moved to London fr   ...as co-host of
Hammer & Tongue and created Siren Says, a regular event which
encourages new young poets onto the stage and culminates in a
slam during the Bristol Poetry Festival. James works in PR and
writes a poetry column for Huffington Post UK.

Jack Dean is an MC, poet and a former Bard of Bath. He took his
well received one man show *Under Stokes Croft* on tour during
2012 and according to Tom Morris (Creative Director of Bristol
Old Vic and the original co-director of War Horse) Jack is an artist
who "makes us excited about what he might do next". In 2012
Jack launched the National Team Poetry Slam. He is General
Manager of The Bike Shed theatre in Exeter.

RHYMING THUNDER

The Alternative Book Of Young Poets

Edited by
James Bunting & Jack Dean

Burning Eye

This edition published by Burning Eye Books 2012

www.burningeye.co.uk

@burningeye

ISBN 978 1 90913 603 8

Printed by Bell & Bain Ltd., Glasgow

MIX
Paper from
responsible sources
FSC® C007785
FSC
www.fsc.org

CONTENTS

INTRODUCTIONS

JAMES BUNTING

I once read a call for submissions for an anthology of young poets that required all poets to have been born since 1970. People born since 1970 could be grandparents by now; they remember the fall of the Berlin Wall; they were alive when John Lennon and Bob Marley died. I'm not saying they're old, per se, but calling them 'young poets' seems to rather miss the point. If young poets are 42 year olds, then the established poets that are thrust into the public eye and into the school books of kids are still no further from the dusty old clichés of poetry than they ever were.

In not so recent years there has been a surge in poets getting up onto stages and reciting poems like monologues, doing things with words that actors and play-writes never got to do, switching audiences on to the possibilities of poetry. The time of reading from books has passed and the poetry world is being lit up by the mouths and voices of people who want to stand on stages and catch the ears of audiences with as much the words they write as they way they read them. This surge has yet to hit the publishing world and every day I ask myself why.

The poets who use social media, blogs, YouTube, Soundcloud and a host of other social channels to share their work are the same poets who tirelessly travel the country to light up stages in front of hundreds of people who have discovered what poetry has become. Those are the poets who people should be talking about, who should be selling out theatres and getting 5 star reviews, those are the poets we should be labelling 'young'.

That is what brings us here. Not to raise the flag of performance poetry in a Stage versus Page war, but to give another side to the story; to offer up the voices of people who have won acclaim from audiences before critics, and from the people who actually got to experience their talent first hand and understand why they are so important.

This book isn't about "getting people in to poetry", it's not about railing against the establishment, it's about showing that poetry isn't the reserve of Oxbridge professors with elbow patches, but is alive and well in the hearts, the minds, and the mouths of an entire generation. A young generation.

We've brought 21 of the brightest voices of this generation together in this book in a way that has never been done before. It is by no means an exhaustive list of the talent out there, but if you want to understand why people will pack out rooms just to hear someone talking then it's a pretty good place to start, to be inspired and moved, and to eventually go out there and join those people who, night upon night flock to pubs, bars, theatres, cafes, and libraries to hear the poems you are about to read, performed.

These are the poets you don't just need to know about, you want to know about. They are powerful, intelligent, witty, shrewd, observant, out-spoken, politicised, funny, moving, bittersweet, gifted, and, above all, they are young.

JACK DEAN

Words are very important to me. Their creative as well as destructive potential has interested me since I was very small. In my English Literature class at school my friends and I would try and take analytical terms and flip the meanings in a Call My Bluff-type game, mostly, since we were seventeen and mostly virgins, into cheap innuendos: "your mum has litotes... in the face", "you're anally retentive Jake... you retain people's anuses" etc.

When I started rapping, I realised that similar transformations were necessary, as words had to be stretched to breaking point to fit with rigorous rhythmic and rhyming structures (it also always helps to start verses with "yo" and end them with "muthafucka" if possible for added authenticity). Words when spoken, then, undergo an alchemical process, first in the gap between the speaker's brain and the words themselves, and then the one between the words and the listeners ear, the meanings and ideas behind them often rapidly switching along what Saussure called their "associative relations". In the realms of speech in particular, communication occurs both literally and figuratively through movement, of tongues, of sound waves and of definitions. It exists in a hinterland between people where little is concrete or mathematically sensible.

I say all of this because I am worried about words and how they are used. The play and fun of words that has historically been the result of this unavoidable linguistic ambiguity seems too often now to be superseded by strategic, almost weaponised usage. Advertisers, shoddy journalists and political propagandists use words as cudgels, harnessing great reams of vocabulary to hammer home insinuated precepts. I could, for example, tell you that this book is innovative, diverse or challenging, but these terms have all been manhandled and mass-produced so much in recent times as to make you want to use the pages to hit me in the face rather than read them. I am writing at a time where there is a "Big Society" that has no money, a "Cultural Olympiad" where no-one wins or loses, and a "Poet Laureate" who, for being the best in their field in the entire nation, gets to write about the Queen and drink sherry. Clearly the way we communicate is under threat.

With this in mind, I will instead say what the poems in this book are not: they are not going to help you get laid. It is not likely they will be used in any exams or splayed across TV screens to exhort you to get a new phone. They will not necessarily bear great analysis or be charged with subcutaneous information, since poetry is not obliged to be a code. Most importantly, they are not trying to be cleverer than you. Take away titles such as "performance poet", "spoken word artist" or "live literature maker", and what you have left is a bunch of people who have, by saying them out loud, tried to make words exciting for their own sake again. We just scooped them out of back rooms, bars and festival tents and made them write it down. Did it work? Decide for yourself. Muthafucka.

THE POETS

VANESSA KISUULE

Vanessa Kisuule is a performance poet, student and sandwich composition expert based in Bristol. She has been performing up and down the country for two years, saying words that sometimes rhyme but sometimes don't. She has won several slams including Farrago School's Out Slam Champion 2010, Bang Said The Gun, Poetry Rivals 2011, Next Generation Slam 2012, and SLAMbassadors 2010. She has performed at Glastonbury, Lounge on the Farm, Secret Garden Party Wilderness and Shambala Festival and performed alongside Linton Kwesi Johnson, Kate Tempest, Dizraeli and David J. She has also performed in pubs, cafes, back gardens, kitchens and once blagged her way out of a bus fare through the power of poetry. No word of a lie.

CRAYON

The kid holds a crayon like a last chance;
I ask what he's drawing and he quickly shakes his head;
I suddenly realise the irrelevance of the question,
He does not put things into boxes yet.
He does not prop up the corners of his smile with insincerity yet.
His Playdoh heart hasn't furled into a fist of fear yet.
The crayon hasn't been seized from his clammy palms
He hasn't been told to colour inside the lines.
Not yet.
Dot to dots are just suggestions to him
Round like the peas
He refuses to eat at dinner time,
Finite like the full stops on the ends
Of prison sentences.
He sees past their constellation of conformity,
Anarchy forming wobbly lines
Like sugared skipping ropes at playtime.
Not even the paper will tell him where his boundaries are.
His crayon scribbles its joy past the A4 and across the table,

Waxy trails in the grooves of the wooden desk,
He switches to felt tips and inks the ends of Nora's pigtails
And gingham dress
A Crayola shade of chaos that I ought to have stopped long ago
Had the knot of envy in my stomach not been so tight.
His tongue rests in the gap where his front teeth once were
As he grins a grin that could turn dust into glitter:
"You can't do that, kid." I tell him.
I hand him a fresh sheet of paper,
A sharpened HB pencil,
I follow the numbered dots with lines sharp as scissor blades,
He takes the pencil and copies me
Diligently.
I walk back to my desk and pick up my pen
Fighting the urge to bite into my skin
Scribble all over the magnolia walls
Remember when Crayon wax collected underneath my
        fingernails
As if I had gripped the world with both hands
And refused to let go.

JJAJJA (Luganda for Grandma)

I do not know you;
I have composed you from
Dress cotton,
Banana leaves,
Patchwork quilts of quiet smiles and stories
That I could not understand
As I hold your hands.
I know they've known more work in this past hour
Than mine will in their entire lifespan.
I see the hardship of a thousand winds that have blown across
        your face
So, I trace a map of apologies across the fault lines of your
        fingers
And hope some amorphous ghost of my meaning lingers.

18

You're a goddess,
I see your shoulder blades press together
Where your wings once met
And yet
We can only exchange awkward nods of acknowledgement
Because my world cannot slot into yours
Though I crawl on all fours for meagre scraps of my identity,
Endlessly grieving every mistranslation,
Misunderstanding,
Misinterpretation,
Each seismic shift in time
I'm inventing you
Through a generation gone by.

And as we sit in silence,
Seedlings of the same wizened tree,
I can imagine
I'd tell you of the short skirts girls in England wear,
And the joys of Jeremy Kyle,
How snow falls like capricious cotton balls of bliss
On nights cold as an Eskimo's kiss.
I'd ask of the past,
The laughter shared,
The songs once sung,
What Mum was like when she was young,
If I weren't trapped with the handicap of my British tongue.

I envision the talks we'd have
Tucked in the candlelit cave of a power cut,
Cradled in a clash of culture
Hoping the Tower of Babel might bleed into oblivion
And somehow
A tainted miracle might unfurl.
I'm willing to bet we'd have been the best of friends
In a different world.

But I do not know you;
I've composed you from
Dress cotton,

Banana leaves,
Patchwork quilts of quiet smiles and stories
That I could not understand.
In this land of lost language I am neither stranger nor native;
The weight of my wasted words cannot be translated.

STRAWBERRIES

Strawberries always remind me of you.
Sweet, red flesh of squandered summer days;
The bizarre novelty of the word boyfriend tingling on my lips.
There were plums, rhubarb and raspberries on your parents'
        farm,
Ripe and blushing like a bride slowly and softly undressed
But I liked the strawberries the best.
I'd eat them by the punnetful and always felt sick afterwards,
I gorged on them so that when their season ended
I wouldn't miss them so much.

I was sixteen then and my virgin lips had yet to be kissed,
I felt like a freak floating face down in a jet black abyss –
P.S. Thanks for pulling me out.
You were ever so white and small and skinny
We looked silly together but I didn't care
Because when I spoke you listened,
As if my voice were the chorus to your favourite song
And your lovely eyes more than made up for your lanky arms.
You'd read a lot of books and knew a lot of stuff
That was enough for me,
You were like my teacher –
One that I could make out with
Behind rhododendron bushes at house parties.

But we argued incessantly,
Mainly over whether Bob Dylan or Aretha Franklin
Were the more superior artist.
I was stood in Aretha's corner

Holding up her heavenly wail of molten gold
Like a shield of sheer unadulterated awesomeness.
You retaliated by making me listen to Dylan,
Some anaemic hunk of a hippy
Who wore Rayban shades indoors
And had a voice that made me crave Strepsils:
"Bob Dylan," I said, "is a glorified poet with delusions of
        musicianship."
"Aretha Franklin," you said, "never wrote a note of what she
        sang.
She had mediocre albums and occasional hits."
It was an argument rendered obsolete
By how fundamentally different the two are –
The underlying metaphor was lost on us –
But I didn't budge and you didn't budge
And now we're just friends who talk occasionally,
And I listen to *Blowin' In The Wind* constantly,
Not so much because I miss you
But more because I can now concede that sometimes I'm wrong,
That sometimes I'm difficult and cruel and obstinate,
Unwilling to let 'like' ferment into other 'l' words.
I was constantly comparing what we had
To what I'd seen in movies,
And heard in songs,
And read in Shakespearean sonnets,
And our adolescent ambivalence always fell short.
When we kissed I simulated the sensation of my heart skipping
        a beat,
It almost felt real.
But I wanted 'crush' to be an operative word,
All the clichés bursting into Technicolor and pushing me to my
        knees,
I wanted to feel your hands clasped round the rungs of my
        ribcage
Holding on for dear life.
I wanted my stomach to ache when you weren't with me
Like an overexcited child that's eaten too many strawberries.
Strawberries always remind me of you,
And how I'll always be writing 'like' poems

And 'lust' poems
And 'what was all that fuss' poems.
Never love poems.
But that's not your fault or mine,
Blame Hollywood,
Blame high hopes,
Blame Motown's marshmallow rhymes.

And though we're no longer together,
And your voice is fainter than a whisper,
Across a barren field in bleakest winter
I still imagine, against all odds,
Bob and Aretha sat on a bench somewhere
Singing in perfect harmony
Their voices melding into endless possibilities
As they share a punnet of big, red, juicy strawberries.

SH'MAYA

Sh'maya is a Brixton-based poet making fresh waves through London's spoken word and slam scene. His writing is filled with deep spiritual honesty, Jazz rhythms and tales of the city. He has performed alongside the greats of London's Poetry and Jazz scene, performing at such venues as The Borderline, Rich Mix and Ronnie Scott's Jazz club. For a significant period of his childhood, his favourite, and constant, piece of clothing was a pair of lederhosen that his grandparents brought back from the Austrian Alps.

CANTICLE

when I am ready to write you
when I have found the words
I need
I will take a train to Victoria Station
and head South
walk past Westminster
walk past Parliament
to the banks of the Thames
where the walls are stained grey
by the smoke of a million passing ships

there I will etch my poems to you
turn each brick into a sonnet
each tower into a book
each rooftop a volume

take Waterloo Bridge
dress it in words ultra violet
write in molten light
so as to print my ink on the back of eyelids
turn shut-eyes into skylights
and irises to spiders on fire

birth visions mid-blinks
spin subliminal pictures
through the pits of spirits
to flicker as wings
unhinge galaxies tilting
on the verge of birth
unearth the thirst of deserts
held buried in vessels
laid as seed long before the soil of time
who cry for the springs of Elim
the pools of Eden
the light of candles burning
for the prayers of the sky
that die as desire
rise as white tridents
pierce hearts
bleed deaths
raise life
through ocean chambers
evoked in the flight of your cries

where spines become vined in lightning
budding
schools of thought
rooms of knowledge
wombs of new covenants
spun from the blood of
dawns uncovered
in the vaults of white dwarves
where aurora forms
as horses roaring
through rivers of wine
sliding down the throats of pens
you set dancing
across the pages
of my need

when I find the words
this is how I'll write them

until that time
I'll scratch away in notepads
and back alleys
take comfort from the fact that one day
I may take a train to Victoria Station
head South
past Westminster
past Parliament
to where your pages will be waiting

{   }

I asked you once what the most beautiful word was;
you told me to close my eyes
so you could show me
the strains of the world.

When I opened them again
we were on the streets of Marrakech,
where the dust was as dry as an ocean unwept.
We found a man in a market selling china cups.
He held one to us and said:
at night these look like swans
floating on the dusk,
and when you turn them to the moonlight
you can drink the stars.
There is no word as vast as

{Porcelain}

We were cast to the shore of a Kenyan beach,
where the childless woman stood like a vase,
feet wet in the night,
hands stretched to a waiting womb.
As her eyes turned to ours,
she spoke to the tide:

This hope is life,
a bird set free.
Pulled the sleeve of her blouse,
showed the word

{Yearn}

as henna on her wrist.
There is none more beautiful than this,
she whispered,
as her eyes turned to silence
in the wreathes of the night.

We fell through her tears,
moved to the benches of Moscow,
where an old man sat.
He told us to hold out our hands,
skin flat to the sky,
to let the white land
and melt to our heat.
To count each flake
and feel the hush.
How each second passing
is one closer to death.
The word that forms my every breath is

{Birth}

There is none with worth like this.

We were spun to the slums of Delhi,
traded bread with beggars
for the breath of their thoughts.

One such man, worn and weary,
spoke deepest of them all.
My friends,
I have seen a million suns rise

on the parchment of these streets.
I have seen its literature written
with the blood of men
and the tears of angels.
I have thought things too great for words,
have drained every possibility from this mind.
I have filled libraries with my questions,
and thus my dreams are empty.
Yet one word fills every corner of my sleep;
It is this one you seek:

{Come}

We were undone to the forests of Bavaria,
to the porch of a cabin
where a logman sat.
Held in his hands was a fallen branch,
undressed and cut by the blade of his knife.
This wood tells stories.
Every line is a rhythm,
every pattern is a dream.
There's a song in every door frame,
a journey in every beam.
He spoke of the voices of the forest
and the way leaves fall,
and as he finished he held up his craft:
the word

{Silence}

etched wet into the flesh of the wood.

Next we stood on the edge of Times Square,
made our way to a cafe
and sat with our thoughts.
There, a waitress
brought us coffee and as we talked,
slipped a folded note beneath the cups.

It read:
My life is built from snapshots;
faces and voices
that never return.
I once saw a man who looked like my father.
The word you want for is

{Somewhere}

as she disappeared
on the wings of an Atlantic storm.

We were flung to the decks
of an ocean trawler,
soaked in the salt of unending waves.
Crouched in the hub of the bow
was a sailor
who beckoned us to the cover
of a canvas sheet.
Then he started to speak:
I have warred a thousand oceans,
battled the rage of the wildest squalls.
I have lost life to the wrath of nature,
seen sights that have caused me to be born again.
Once I saw a girl in a cove in St Lucia,
where the sea was as still as the blue of her eyes.
Her skin was like copper
and her name was

{Glimmer}

It is this word that comes in the watches of the night;
the word I cradle in my arms
like the warmth of her flesh.
No man could utter a sweeter breath,
he wept
as we fell through the depths of a deeper ocean.
We came to the playgrounds of London,

made our way to the quietest child,
lost in the noise
of a world she couldn't understand,
gave her our hands,
let her trace her thoughts
on the flesh of our palms,
'til she beckoned us closer,
spoke the word

{Whisper}

through the mist of our ears.

We travelled like this for years,
searched every corner
of every land,
gathered passions in our pockets
and questions in our bags,
until one night
we found a cave by a sea
where the moonlight
coloured the walls like
rain.

Here we found it,
quivering like a foal
beneath the folds of a rock.
You caught it up in your arms
and held it like a child,
tears dressing your cheeks
like the years we'd lost.
You gave it to me,
its breath on your kiss

{   }

I felt a sun rise in my chest.
You told me to close my eyes

so you could show me
the strains of the world.

WITNESSES

Where we came from
the lands we've known
the things we've done

witnesses witnesses

caught between moonshine
and streetlight
tangled in flame
in flesh
making love in dreams
of stars
waking
heart burning
for faceless glory
giving birth
in hands unfurled
having birth given

witnesses brothers
witnesses sisters
the things we've done
the lands we've known

caught glimpses of angels in
high street windows
caught glimpses of trembling cities
of children unborn
of cities unwritten
of hands yet held
held counsel with Heavenly beings in Brixton backyards
touched cherubim

in the eyes of beggars
cathedrals
in the sighs of the broken
plunged hands into holy scriptures
eyes into lines between
emerged glistened on London streets
on New York streets
Cape Town
Moscow
Calcutta
Baghdad
Wastelands
Playgrounds
Rooftops
Basements
skinned knees on wanton floors
wept speech marks
from eyelids
scrawled note pads books papers lovers
with the ink of our tears
chalked haikus on pavements
pressed handprints on windows
prayed they'll turn to
voices for the poor
beds for the weary
dawns for the barren
truth for the hungered

rubbed shoulders with fear
tore ashes tore sackcloth of fear
shared beds with desolation
shared bread with lies
shared shelter with questions
shared tables with critics
the critics
we tamed in our minds
waged war with our minds
hostaged our minds
routed the minds

of the enemy
learnt our enemy
found our enemy
named our enemy
raised to life the places purged
raised to life the places chained
raised the places undone
the places scorned
the places sought for
in dreams
in dust
in poems
made love in dreams
of stars
woken
heart burning
for faceless glory
given birth
in hands unfurled
had birth given
dared to search
dared to sit with Love
dared to witness Love
dared to touch Love's wounds
dared to let Love touch
dared to know
His name
His face
His words
His witness
of fire
His fire

AMY ACRE

Amy Acre was born in London in 1980. She has performed poetry at spoken word nights, festivals, radio stations, parties, beaches and bus stops. Her work has been published in Poetry Review, South Bank Poetry and Rising, received a commendation from Magma, and won a bunch of slams. She is one fifth of a poetry collective, Dirty Hands. She sees poetry, not as two worlds of page and performance, but as a spectrum. Her aim is to trip along that spectrum with the reckless abandon of a student at an all-you-can-eat buffet.

PREVENTING EARTHQUAKES

You hold yourself in place with tight clips,
never let any loose wave slip through the net,
vet words before they break from your lips,

never trip over your temper,
but temper your talk with charm,
and though you disarm the room,
no skimmed stone can stir the slick of your emotions.
You're frozen in time.
Unflappable, unflammable despite belly fire.

You aspire to be phlegmatic,
to keep static when others panic,
to banish irregular beats of the heart to the attic of your chest.

You are the still surface lilies rest upon.
You reflect, but don't warm to the spots where sun shone.
Your secretions that secretly rise in their legions
may glottal stop your oesophagus –
but won't drop from your eyes 'til I'm gone.

You take all reasonable measures to prevent earthquakes.

You are the intransigent land beneath which magma boils.
You do not respond to the drilling of oil,

but sometimes intrepid feet slip through your soil
and bring light seeping in to the place
where your passion lies sleeping,

and you're bursting, hurting with the flare of it,
and the fact that your flame turns inwards
doesn't mean I'm unaware of it.

It's whispered in kisses you try to damp down with congestion.
Your innards burn with a fever you swallowed
that gives you indigestion.

If you lose your self-possession,
if you shake off your cloak of protection,
if you awake what lies fallow, and take out your marrow
and leave it exposed to attack,
you could unleash such violent, sparkling tornados
the stars might fall and the sea might crack

because you,
you contain all the fire that lights night skies.

You aspire to be phlegmatic,
but however emphatically you deny your tears,
however deeply you hide the scorching sands that brand your
        years,
however tightly you slam the door that could free you,

I see you.

1.21 GIGAWATTS

Take me back to the future we'll never have.

Take me to your bed sweats and dead end stories
that get lost and end up in Morden.

Steal plutonium from Libyan terrorists.
Leave them a shoddy bomb casing
stuffed with the guts of an old pinball machine.

Give me ornamental sheep and waterlogged teeth
so our kisses
echo.

Set the time circuits twenty years from now
and show me how you midlife crisis.
We'll ride through your fat Elvis years,
your alarming flirtation with crystal healing.

Send cables streaming in a bruise of sky.
Wrap fingers tight round a bolt of lightning.

Show me worthless fights
and you missing my fortieth birthday
to drive Tony to the airport.

Abort the embryos of memories.
Let our thirty-something stalemates wrinkle backwards.
Shed them to powder.

Headbutt the dashboard and tell me
– I should have done you better
– I should never have bought that almanac
– this is all my fault.

Now step into the DeLorean.

Catapult me out of you.

You are twenty-nine.

You make a rift in the continuum.
You erase my timeline,
my face from your photo,
with your insulting lack of infidelity,
with your slap-sharp beauty,
and I feel like a twat
in my matching yellow jumpsuit and helmet.

Take me back to that future we'll never have.

Turn the crank of truth till I'm ready to homewreck
the marriage of cause and effect.

Return to an empty car park
in the shoulder of night,
five unmarked minutes tapping the hour

and tell me it's over.
It's ok.
I'm ready now.

PERCUSSION

I can't do this.

I know it's late.

I know everyone's waiting,
expecting

the thweck of flinging limbs
Fred-Astairing fat sonatas
over snare beats cast in metal,

staccato flesh hits
dripping on floor tiles,

concubine hips that splay
to a Tae Kwon Do kick,
feet flying all around you.

It's just that
I was lying
when I told you I could salsa.

I don't know why I did it.

I guess I thought
this time would be different,
that the Bomba bass
would shoot shock therapy
thunder to my toe touch.
I just wanted to impress you.
I just like you so much.

But now guillotine beats
drop fast and precise,
hope bristles and burns
in your Christmas Eve eyes
and I have to admit

it's all been lies.
My thighs can't twist
the way you want them to.

I'm English

and I'm far from double-jointed.
At the end of all this,
you'll only wind up disappointed.

Trying to be kind
as I trip off the stage,
you'll say it's a brave
interpretation of the rhythm.

When I elbow you in the neck,
you'll tell me pleasure
can't exist without pain.

You'll grow increasingly aware
of the way my knees disagree with each other
as habitually
as an old married couple.

You'll hold me closer
to block out the guilt
as you look longingly over my shoulder
at *Strictly*.

You'll decorate dance floors
with furtive glances that ask,
'are we the worst couple in the room, again?'
and by then you'll know

I can't be the reason you smile.
I can't catch you and spin you round.
I'll only get caught up in loose carpet
and knock picture frames to the ground.

As night falls down, you'll lie there
feeling like Mother Theresa,
Florence Nightingale,
thinking of the big karmic bonus
you're racking up with every
step, turn and kiss.

You'll be so miserable
you'll think I must be happy
because fuck knows
one of us has to be.

I can't do this.

I can't be the slipstream percussion

that slips around but won't
puncture your heart.

I'm sorry,
but I just can't.

HARRY BAKER

Harry is London, UK, European and World Poetry Slam Champion, with two 5 Star Edinburgh fringe shows under his belt. He has performed internationally including in Chicago, New York, Munich, and Warsaw. Harry is currently studying for a Maths degree in term time and doing the festival circuit in summer. He is living the dream.

PAPER PEOPLE

I like people.
I'd like some paper people.
They'd be purple paper people.
Maybe pop up purple paper people.
Proper pop up purple paper people.
"How do you prop up pop up purple paper people?"
I hear you cry. Well I...

I'd probably prop up proper pop up purple paper people
with a proper pop up purple people paperclip,
but I'd pre-prepare appropriate adhesives as alternatives,
a cheeky pack of blu tack just in case the paper slipped.
I could build a pop up metropolis.
but I wouldn't wanna deal with all the paper people politics.
Paper politicians with their paper-thin policies,
broken promises without appropriate apologies.

There'd be a little paper me, and a little paper you,
and we'd watch paper TV and it would all be paper view.
We'd watch the poppy paper rappers rap about their paper
          package
or watch paper people carriers get stuck in paper traffic on the
          A4.
There'd be a paper princess Kate but we'd all stare at paper
          Pippa,

and then we'd all live in fear of killer Jack the Paper-Ripper.
'Cause the paper propaganda propagates the people's prejudices,
papers printing pictures of the photogenic terrorists.

There'd be a little paper me, and a little paper you,
but in a pop up population people's problems pop up too.
There'd be a pompous paper parliament who remained out of
        touch,
and who ignored the people's protests about all the paper cuts,
then the peaceful paper protests would get blown to paper
        pieces,
by the confetti cannons manned by pre-emptive police.

There would still be paper money, so there'd still be paper
        greed,
and the paper piggy bankers pocketing more than they need.
Purchasing the potpourri to pepper their paper properties,
while others live in poverty and ain't acknowledged properly,
a proper poor economy where so many are proper poor,
but while their needs are ignored the money goes to big wars.
Origami armies unfold plans for paper planes
we remain imprisoned by our own paper chains,
and the greater shame, is that we always seem to stay the same,
what changes is who's in power choosing how to lay the blame,
they're naming names, forgetting these are names of people,
cause in the end it all comes down to people.

I like people. Because even when the situation's dire,
it is only ever people who are able to inspire,
and on paper – it's hard to see how we all cope,
but in the bottom of pandora's box there's still hope,
and I still hope 'cause I believe in people.
People like my grandparents.
Who every single day since I was born have taken time out of
their morning to pray for me.
That's 7398 days straight of someone checking I'm okay and
        that's amazing.
People like my aunt who puts on plays for prisoners.
People who are capable of genuine forgiveness.

People who go out of their way to make your life better and
        expect nothing in return.
People have potential to be powerful.
and just because the people in power tend to pretend to be
        victims,
we don't all need to succumb to the system.
A paper population is no different.

There'd be a little paper me and a little paper you,
and we could watch paper TV and it would all be paper view,
and in a pop up population people's problems pop up too,
but even if the whole world fell apart then we'd still make it
        through -
because we're people.

REAL MEN

I am a man.
Sometimes I put my manhood on display,
like going skinny dipping in the sea on New Year's Day.
I've gone up for thirds in an all-you-can-eat buffet
and I have not once worried about how much I weigh.

I am a man.
Sometimes I do manly things,
not to prove I am a man, but that's just part of what it brings.
So when I stay up playing FIFA on my PS3 till 4,
it's not because I'm insecure, it's 'cause it's fun.

And some say, that real men are brave men,
and brave men are cave men,
and cave men are men who do not really show emotion.
I say if something is real, it's something you can feel,
and that could be love, religion, fear or uncertainty.

Because real men have issues, and real men cry,
That's why they make man-sized tissues for their man-sized eyes.

And I cry quite a lot.
And in this day and age,
whether a man's eyes are dry or not determines that he may be
gay...
But I am not.
I like a girl, I just cry like a girl at certain things.
My main form of catharsis is Pixar flicks.
The reason that I see them in the cinema is
so you cannot see my tears behind those 3D glasses.
Because I broke down in Up.
I wept in Toy Story 3.
I was on the brink in Monsters Inc. and Cars did the same thing
to me.
When watching Wall-E I wasn't worried about which of my
friends' willies was bigger,
because something in the animation pulled an emotional trigger,
and you may snigger, if you see my guns are not the manliest
but I figure that ain't the best way to measure manliness.

Because real men have issues, and real men cry,
that's why they make man-sized tissues –
not to be misused by never-been-kissed youths in dimly lit rooms
searching YouTube for big boobs,
but for the man-sized tears that run from man-sized eyes.
and the last one I used was watching Sky News when the story
came through of a kid named Jordan Rice in Australia,
in the worst floods in years, which reduced many men to floods
of tears.
When faced with death, he didn't hesitate or take a breath, just
gave his life for his brother.
So I cried for the brother who died for another, aged 13.
The age a boy steps into manhood,
he proved that he could fill his boots as well as any man could,
because real men are brave, right?

Well it don't get much braver.
So yes, I am 19,
I'm not the most prolific shaver.
If anything I only really weekly need a razor,

maybe bi-weekly.
And not as in twice weekly,
as in once every two weeks, maybe even longer.
Sometimes I am too weak and I wish I could be stronger.
I did Movember and nobody even noticed
but, know this...

I am a man.
As are about half of you,
regardless who has been doing press-ups all afternoon,
and when I was 13,
I'd stand on my head until the sky was green
and the grass was blue,
then somewhere on this path I grew.
So yeah I'm still a kid at heart and not ready to grow up
and when I go to Nando's I drink too much coke and throw up
but here's something that we can raise those refillable glasses to,
because growing up is something not every kid gets a chance to
        do.

THE SUNSHINE KID

Old man sunshine was proud of his sun,
and it brightened his day to see his little boy run,
not because of what he'd done,
nor the problems overcome,
but that, despite that, his disposition remained a sunny one.
It hadn't always been like this.
There'd been times when he'd tried to hide his brightness,
every star hits periods of hardship,
it takes a brighter light to inspire them through the darkness.
If we go back to when he was born in a nebula,
we know that he never was thought of as regular,
because he had a flair about him,
to say the Midas touch is wrong
but all he went near seemed to turn a little bronze.
Yeah this sun was loved by some more than others,

It was a case of Joseph and his dream-coat and his brothers –
standing out from the crowd had its pros and its cons,
and jealousy created enemies in those he outshone,
such as the Shadow People.

Now the Shadow People didn't like the Sunshine Kid,
because he showed up the dark things the Shadow People did,
and when he shone he showed the places where
the Shadow People hid.
So the Shadow People had an evil plan to get rid of him.
First up – they made fun of his sunspots,
shooting his dreams from the sky, their words were gunshots,
designed to remind him he wasn't very cool,
and he didn't fit in with any popular kids at school.
They said his head was up in space and they would bring him
                    down to earth,
essentially, he came from nothing and that is what he was
                    worth.
He'd never get to go to university to learn,
the only degrees he'd ever show would be the 1st degree burns
from those that came too close, they told him he was too bright,
that's why no-one ever looked him in the eye.
His judgement became clouded and so did the sky,
with evaporated tears as the sun started to cry.

The sunshine kid was bright, with a warm personality,
but inside he burned savagely –
hurt by the words and curses of the shadowy
folk who spoke holes in his soul and left cavities,
and as his heart hardened,
his spark darkened.

Every time they called him names it cooled his flame.
He thought they might like him if he kept his light dim,
but they were busy telling lightning she had terrible aim.
He couldn't quite get to grips with what they said,
so he let his light be eclipsed by what they said.
He fell into a Lone Star State like Texas,
and felt like he'd been punched in his solar plexus.

That's when Little Miss Sunshine came along,
singing her favourite song
about how we're made to be strong,
and you don't have to be wrong to belong,
just be true to who you are,
because we are all stars at heart.
Little miss sunshine was hot stuff –
the kind of girl when you looked at her you forgot stuff,
but for him, there was no forgetting her.
The minute he saw her her image burned in his retina.
She was out of this world, and she accepted him.
Something about this girl meant he knew whenever she was
         next to him,
things weren't as dark as they seemed,
and he dared to dream,
shadows were nowhere to be seen;
when she was there he beamed.
His eyes would light up in ways that can't be faked,
when she grinned her rays erased the razor-tipped words of
         hate.
They gave each other nicknames –
they were 'cool star' and 'fun sun',
and gradually the shadowy damage became undone.
She was one in a septillion,
and she was brilliant,
could turn the coldest blooded reptilian vermillion,
loved by billions,
from Chileans to Brazilians,
and taught the Sunshine Kid the meaning of resilience.

She said:
"All the darkness in the world cannot put out the light of a single
candle,
so how the hell can they handle your light?
Only you can choose to dim it,
and the sky is the limit,
so silence the critics
by burning."
If eyes are windows to the soul then she drew back the curtains

46

and let the sunshine through the hurting.
In a universe of adversity two stars stuck together,
and though day becomes night the memories last forever,
whether the weatherman said it or not, it would be fine,
'cause even behind the clouds the kid could still shine.
The Sunshine Kid was bright, with a warm personality,
and inside he burned savagely,
fuelled by the fire inspired across galaxies,
by the girl who showed him belief.

JODI ANN BICKLEY

Jodi Ann Bickley has a beautiful heart. She has quietly become one of the country's most loved spoken word artists. She has collaborated with Skream (Magnetic Man), Brackles (Rinse FM) and Shlomo (Mouthronica) and has performed everywhere from mates' living rooms to Glastonbury. She also runs Birmingham's loveliest Spoken Word night, Speak Up, and would love to see you there.

UNIT

We sat in silence. Not because we had nothing to say – we both had so much to say but we knew anything we said – nothing could change. Mobile phones in palms for four hours. I could tell you exactly what my heart tasted like. I could tell you what my Mum's fear smelt like – chain smoke masked by vanilla scented candles and Nescafe coffee.

He's out late again, working late again. Her head in hands as I'm checking for sight of headlights through the curtains. Tonight we discussed packing up and running away – in times like these I've learnt that even atheists pray. We have no idea who we were calling but I've never left a more sincere voicemail. Headlights. We both sit upright, turn the TV back on and laugh like we hadn't been cradling each other before you arrived. You place bags of powder into a candle holder I made age nine and I swear in this light you were someone I just didn't recognise. The worst thing is I get it.

Tonight made me want to improve my upper cut and learn to tombstone, words that I'd picked up from wrestling videos we used to watch aged 10 and 7 that the secure homes man would record for us and you'd pretend to be macho man and I'd be Lex Luger and you'd say I couldn't be on your team because you had to fight your own battles and I understood because back then our

48

fights were between 30cm plastic figurines in a pretend wrestling ring. But it's different now.

I want to carry you in my pockets in hope you'd hear something in the praise I bestow on you when we're apart, to realise you are the most precious thing in the world and I know that's not a very cool thing to say out loud so I won't but I would if you'd just listen. I want to record your laugh when we're together so you remember that home is where the heart is and going back to where you started doesn't mean you are a loser it means you know a good thing when you've got it.

If you want to just sit, we can do that. You can have the remote and I won't moan when you watch those scrapheap shows because now I kind of like them even though I'll never admit that because then you might up it a notch. Tonight you talked about getting a stab proof vest in all seriousness. In an area where cutlery is as common under pillows and in pockets as in kitchen drawers.

I got in the passenger seat as Mum drove me back to Kings Heath. Mum had her phone out before we even pulled off as a shifty guy came storming up the middle of the road – car doors locked. Turned and walked off, drunk or just an absolute lunatic – did a drug deal a couple of houses down, where we used to play out until that sign went up saying no ball games allowed.

UP IN THE CLOUDS.

I should of known that something which began and ended in the same room would never last outside of it. As someone who is usually quite the escape artist I was willing to stay right there, door locked – curtains wide open at a height that my five year old self would definitely of thought was where the clouds began not where these sort of things happened.

I always wondered why people had sex against walls or on the floor or in lifts instead of a comfier option and realised up here that it happens because you don't realise you're in the lift or against the wall or on the floor. And up here, that was completely fine.

I woke up extra quietly and took you in, time was limited and I know that this moment would be featured in the montage of memories that you go through on those sleepless nights so I needed to get this memory just right. My footsteps left notes in capital letters in hope you'd keep me but I soon realised that was ridiculous so retraced each step and left a "Thanks for visiting" postcard beside the bed.

I didn't hold myself in any higher regard to consider being anything more than a ship in the night, you hated that but I knew a discussion of my self esteem was definitely not something I wanted to do with the time that we had left. I made tea like a ninja and tucked myself onto a window sill with a view of a place that the mention of in future would only remind me of you.

I was closer to the sun than I had ever been so I whispered if she'd give way to the moon, whose shadow was dropping to her right side, just so we had a little bit more time. Thankfully I didn't ask this out loud. The windows were double glazed and I'm sure the sun has a million other things to do than to allocate a little bit more time to me and you. But I sat on the window sill for a while longer and, dare I say it, the moon continued to partly curtain the sun as if to say, look your time isn't up quite yet.

I looked back over to the bed and realised I had no idea what to do with the end of my night before you woke up and morning began. So I moved from the window sill, to the sofa and even contemplated moving all the furniture around just to occupy myself but stopped after minimal changes, instead I put five bubblegums in my mouth and crossed and uncrossed my legs about twenty times before returning back to the window sill and realised that if I continued to put bubblegums in my mouth I would probably choke and die so instead I put my hand over my mouth as if to catch all the words I'm pretty sure would of fell out, woken you up and I would have to explain everything leading up to this point and why the coffee table has now moved to the left side of sofa when last night it was in front of it.

It's weird isn't it. Down there a pairing wasn't a big thing. It wasn't a secret, but I knew without being told that this shouldn't be spoken of. I wondered if each person had to contain their excitement when kissed and whether a hand hold lead to them wanting to shout really loudly "AS IF YOU ARE DOING THAT!". Because I know that I would. We hadn't held hands. I consider holding hands a big thing. And although this was definitely something, I'm not sure the scale of it just yet.

Up here it meant everything but down there each finger space of thought would be filled up with like crossing roads, getting the right coach home, work tonight + other stuff. That up here didn't need to be considered but down there really mattered. I wondered if you'd think about me on the way home or whether you'd leave me somewhere between the sheets and the station. I wondered whether to open the window and breathe out in hope you'd reach the moon so I'd always be twelve hours away from you. You'd be in a place I knew existed but couldn't get to and that would be fine I reckon. I reckon it would be a safer option. Don't you? I do. I wasn't tall enough to reach the latch of the window so instead made a temporary notepad on the glass. I drew a heart, I always draw hearts – it doesn't mean anything I don't think, but someone once told me I was in love with love and it kind of always makes me think of that.

I don't think I am. I wrote your name and then my name and then scribbled it out because the part of me that thinks it's that simple to disregard feeling is regularly beaten to a pulp by the other side of me that knows for a fact that it's never that easy.

I imagined one of the people below were you and watched "you" walk away and didn't understand when it didn't hurt that much and I guessed that maybe I was waiting for you to leave since the minute you got here. We were both here under the pretense, of company and sex – without the awkward forgetting each other's name in the morning bit, the swapping numbers with one wrong digit and the promise of this being anything more than a little something that will in future be symbolised by a look across a room that people will never notice except us two. A secret imprinted on irises, "you'd of had to been there to get it" – "do you fancy him" – don't be stupid. I didn't.

What I was feeling was almost like waking up hanging off the bed. A cabin bed. A really, really high bed and you're either gunna fall hard or pull yourself up, go back to sleep – wake up as if nothing happened and I wasn't quite sure which it was going to be so I convinced myself it was the latter, because it was just kind of safer. The sun had almost beat the moon in the battle for our bit of sky and although I knew it had to happen – I wasn't ready to say goodbye yet. I wasn't ready to be just real good friends again, just yet. I wasn't ready to see you in this light yet. I snuck back to bed, facing the wall – as I'm not sure I was ready for you to see me in this light yet. See me as a good friend again yet, I didn't want you to say bye yet.

You woke up an hour later, friend. And without the starlit backdrop, fight club soundtrack and quickly purchased treats from a closing supermarket – we slipped straight back into the day before yesterday, before our friendly one night stand – numbers already in phone. Texts all the way home. I heard you no longer wake up alone. And it bothered me for a minute.
Like, waking up – hanging off the bed.
Not sure if you're gunna fall
or pull yourself up,
wake up and forget about it.

OLD AND GREY

When we are old and grey I want you to look back and say I couldn't of loved you better. It's a promise, that I definitely could not love anybody more. I want us to dance to old love songs of the legends we grew up with, which for now to my knowledge will definitely be Adele and Ed Sheeran. We will laugh at old TV shows and tell our grandchildren that CSI was not true to life and they should not be worried. I hope by then my predictions are the same. I hope they live in a world a little better than ours that someone along the line has used their powers for good, but to remind them that we will always have it better than others – we are not doing so badly. And then you'd help me up onto my bad knee which I predict I will have because even now my legs hurt going up certain staircases and we would cook for everybody, our family will be massive. And we'll hold it all together – you'll channel Morgan Freeman whilst I'll emulate Helen Mirren and I'll love your impossibility to sound like God and you'll laugh at my lack of grace and I'll remind myself of our lifetimes that are etched into your face, so beautifully. You will have such a hold of me, still.

They'd love your mash potato and I'd never explain that actually you didn't know how to make it before me. How technically your mashed potato is the same as mine, you just leave it clumpy because you get bored half way through. We'd stay up 'til 12 some nights talking about past times, our lives together and what we want to do next. You still have dreams of living on a barge and I haven't had a blue rinse yet. You'd sing Bob Marley at the top of your voice, waking me some mornings only to come downstairs to breakfast made for two and I'm not sure you'll realise how absolutely in love with you I still will be.

You still call me baby and I swear at 78 we will be the cutest couple in the bingo hall. I'll still make you laugh in the middle of serious phone calls and you'll grab my bum in the queue at the post office. I hate that, you know this, but I can't help but smile.

We'd go to Asda to use the mobility scooters and we'd race down the aisle having half of the shopping list each and we could go at the highest of speeds, 7mph – with the power of the elderly everyone would move for me whilst you got stuck picking biscuits to dunk into our tea later on.

We'd watch Friends re-runs and explain that these were made

nearly 100 years ago, imagine. Our grandkids sporting t-shirts with Joey's face on to be "Vintage" – wearing neon to year 2000's parties and TLC played on Classic FM. I'd hand down my massive earrings, you'd pass on your nikes – memories of the nights we'd spent entwined until 5am walking home as the sun rose and I don't suppose we'd of imagined being together for each one every since. Mental, isn't it. I still get goosebumps when you kiss me. You still blush when I say I love you, I still pinch myself sometimes. I am so glad I met you. When we are old and grey. I want to look back and say I couldn't of love you better. It's a promise, I will never love another more.

LIONHEART

Rhael 'LionHeart' Cape first entered the poetry scene in early 2011. He has since won various competitions and slams in London and had his performance poetry aired on TV in the UK, USA and Africa. As Rhyming Thunder went to press he was working on a short film based on his poem, *They Killed A Man Last Night*. He has been described as "raw, passionate and awe inspiring in his poetic vulnerability, constantly challenging your ears". He likes anime. A lot.

PROMISED TOMORROWS

I love tomorrow's distrust,
minutes of misogyny coupled with possibilities of different
      lives,
we strive to
make tomorrow promise our future.
Promise we'll wake up tomorrow with a love that's not powered
      by fear of loneliness,
a mind that's not light-dependant
a day that isn't defined by the night before or the life our eyes
      can't see.
We all have burdens for gravity.

But had we surgeons for such casualties
as being martyrs of our mornings,
promised tomorrows wouldn't seem so memorial.
Each day we get older
we die closer each time we wake.
Bet many couldn't tell me they haven't slept to forget pain.
See, too many times I've wished my tomorrows would promise
      me my dreams.
But bottles of whisky were the
only spirits I could find close enough to a genie in a bottle.

A Rastafarian told me,

"ah promiss his ah cumferrt to ah foool."
So how dumb do we have to be to be comfortable?

I live vicariously through music videos and movie scenes
hoping to feel like a star that doesn't need limelight to shine,
doesn't need hoes to polish their ego
or fans to cool their self esteem.
I wondered why adults call their children stars,
or why those children never see themselves as stars.
Maybe it's because a star shines so bright it can't see its own
          reflection,
or maybe a star has a name that wasn't defined by a race that
          lied about standing on the moon.
It's true I've achieved things that shouldn't be compared to a
          platinum album.
Even though when I touch the mic I make that precious metal
          sing.
True, I don't own my own house yet,
but that fact doesn't house the fact that I've finally found my
          soul home to my own happiness,
finally found a bank account where paying attention to ME
          finds my self worth,
Finally stopped dreaming for a girl to make me whole when
          they have more holes to fill than me.

Believe.

I am but a promise to a fool, and I promised God I wouldn't
          make fools of his followers
promising them things I think the future holds
when the future is like the eyelids of God, the way it holds his
          vision.
I love seeing the eyes of God in the morning,
seeing another morning.
Mourning the morning before mourning the next.
I dread the day my tomorrows are promised, as I wish not to be
          a fool of my today.

CONSUME

It consumes me,
cannibalistic thoughts constipate my complex digestion.
See, food for thought became thoughts for food.
I'm a thought consumed by an idea that gave life to me.
Water on the brain couldn't cure my thirst for insanity,
so when my water broke
I conceived another concept from complex contractions.
I'm saying my cerebellum is pregnant with self inseminating
        thoughts.
Maybe I'm lost in a lost cause.

THE NEXT ONE IS CALLED 'COOL'

As a kid I jus wanted to be cool,
so I'd dress like you.
Pigeon holed my pigeon toes just to step in shallow minded
        shoes.
You shoehorn for perception,
prying eyes like crowbar concepts on scarecrow playing fields.
We ran into the world crying.
That showed the world we were alive.
But with time,
time will tell too many tales like chinese whispers lost in
        translation;
nothing but experience affects the virgin.
People flirting with the idea,
"U only live once, have fun, party! Get drunk and wake up
beside a girl who had parts of u in her mouth more than she's
        had ur name or compliments."

But I've died too many times with healthy lungs.
I just wanted to be cool,
but cold hearts seek heat so they grow colder,
knowing it burns others who trust enough to touch.
I just wanted to be cool.

But the temperature in this room,
this tomb,
this womb called give me life,
these interactions with those who fought to swim,
they just wanted to be cool,
so they copied your grin and found falsity for scaffolding.
Most people we see as cool see fiery fumes coming from their
        over heated self esteem.
Are we not just thermometers seeking the right temperament in
        life so we can just be cool.

JESSIE DURRANT

A self-styled lyrical rebel, Jessie Durrant strings together rhymes
with passion and conviction. She wants to make you feel her pain
and joy with every beat of her verse. Jessie only began
performing in 2011 but her confident style has earned her a
growing reputation beyond her home town of Cambridge and
she looks set for big things in the future.

A BOY I USED TO KNOW

You told me look up,
because looking down was never enough.
See, there's all this beauty just above our heads,
but we are looking down at the ground instead
and you said:
Look knowledge is power you can sit there and cower
or flower and empower and take each hour like it's your last
but never stay too long in the past.
You're prancing along with a skip in your step,
not one you could easily forget
but then weeks pass, months pass
and now it's a year and a half.
See losing touch with you was my biggest regret but *you* I will
          never forget.
now you walk through these winding streets pale faced,
cheeks sucked in, acting shady and far too fucking thin.
See, you got lost on that rocky road and the smoke it took you in,
because you had it bad mate they really did you in.

And how can I begin to describe quite how much me myself I
          despise.
See, I hate that I wasn't there when all you really needed was
          someone to show that they care but life is far from fair.
And now you pile it in and smoke it up,
choke it up and try your luck,

toke it through to get to you,
unravel and undo to make it true,
leave you lungs black and blue,
until there's nothing left of the boy I knew.

See, you used to be so full of life,
we would stay up all night chatting shite,
talking about how the future was bright.
We would go out and take on the night fists up ready to fight
and now it makes me sad when I see you,
because like a ghost I can see right through you.
Eyes that once sparkled now glazed over,
I mean I'd be surprised if I caught you sober.
But this isn't it man it can't be over,
you have so much left to be if only you could see that it is still a
        possibility.
Because you could have had it all,
but you stumbled and there was no one to catch you fall.
Now you're like an empty shell,
the silence after the ring of the bell,
But ah the stories of you I could tell!
See after the first night I met you I knew I would never forget
        you,
but me I never thought I'd let you slip through and I never
        thought they'd get you.
And now you pile it in and smoke it up,
choke it up and try your luck,
toke it though to get to you,
unravel and undo to make it true,
leave your lungs black and blue until there's nothing left of the
        boy I knew.
Because it happened so fast and I thought our friendship would
        last,
but you were too hungry for that blast.

If only we could go back to the past and restart tell it straight
        from the heart,
instead of letting it grate, manipulate and inhabit your entire
        state.

60

I just hope that you realise before it's too late,
Because you could be something mate you could be great but
        why wait?
Waiting for what?
Your lungs to give up and your bones to rot,
Just another one that time forgot.
This is exactly why this has to stop,
I'm not going to sit back to watch you drop because our
friendship was more than a lot.
But now you pile it in and smoke it up,
choke it up and try your luck,
toke it through to go to you,
unravel and undo to make it true,
leave your lungs black and blue,
until there's nothing left of the boy I knew,
and now there's nothing left of the boy I knew.

BEHIND THE PAINT

It was Trafalgar Square where I saw them there,
he had sleek hair and she was fair but her smile was bare.
And the little girl had perfect curls,
not a smudge of dirt on her face walking hand in hand with her
        parents at such a passive pace.
No one muttering, "what a disgrace!"
See, to me this is an alien race because I come from a place
            where you have got to slap a smile on your face because
            time is not there to waste.
But I had to double-take, as if my eyes had made a mistake.
Such a perfect family it must be fake.
I stare and compare hoping I will find some clarity there but my
        mind is left bare.

And now they are looking at me funny, afraid of my stare, as if
        to say,
"What's this and who goes there."
But I'm too intoxicated to care, so I continue my stare which

transforms into a glare and with a single flare the phantom family
       flee.
I'm left thinking "fuck! Is it me that's the alien and that this is
       normality?
Is this how a family should be?"
Well, its never been that way for me, but this is how I see:
My friends are my family and my family are my friends,
even when we bitch and fight we always make amends,
we don't play fake and pretend.
And this family they look like they have stepped out a
       catalogue,
But I bet they have a whole backlog
of unanswered questions and problems that vex them.
And no, I don't detest them, and I'm not trying to oppress them,
because image is only what you see,
it's not what it is or what it could be, so please,
set your minds free, look a little deeper and you will see,
we all start out the same we just get painted on our portraits
       and given different name and ah, the shame.
See, we get soaked in that poison rain,
we start to fear each other and fight one another, we are hiding
       undercover.
We forget what we could be instead of how we should be.
So, fuck the industry they're what separates us,
and this brass division of class it tears my heart apart.
So what?
We settle with what we know because we are too afraid to grow.
Don't you know, its ok to let your emotion show?
So smile and be happy,
cry and be angry,
because we are human and we are anything we can be.

KAKORRHAPHIOPHOBIA

So, rewind five years and I'm fourteen,
reading Shakespeare on the beach,
sand beneath my feet, life seems sweet.

Just me myself and I, not a single passerby,
so I read it out loud just to see how it sounds,
and it is profound. Like my feet no longer feel the ground,
and I have found meaning in every single syllable I am
        screaming!
Now I'm shouting words into the distance
screaming words into existence not refraining any resistance.
See, I know now what I want to do with my existence.
So I'll write, and I'll write and I'll hold that pen tight,
but there's this constant battle, this endless fight,
this fear in me that's asking me,
"Well, what if I don't get it right?"
The fear of failing in what I believe in, that leave my mind and
        body reeling,
Because I just want to get better with every single letter that I
        spill from my hand through the quill.
See, I have got a need to fulfil.
I want to make people feel; strip it down and make it real; break
        that seal.
I want to get on stage and rain my parade and not be afraid.
Stay up for nights and days just writing,
instead of fighting, writing afraid of getting it wrong.
This has been my song for far too long.
See, I'll get lost and forget where I belong,
but at times we all go wrong it's all about staying head strong.
Because, you'll know when it works.
When your whole body is shaking, when it seems that the whole
        world is trembling and awakening,
when you know that the future is there for the making.
So, let's stop deliberating and start creating,
The whole world is out there just waiting; it's yours for the
        taking!
So, let's get lost in a maze and make it to the middle,
make sense out of every single riddle.
See, its not given to you on a plate.
You have got to build it up slate by slate before it's too little, too
        late.
So, don't just get in a state and let time go to waste,
go try something new, unfold a story that you never knew.

See, there is always something more to learn and millions of
    pages left to turn.
I mean, our lives are not scripted so don't follow the screen play,
you have got to seize it while you can before you start to decay!
See, I am trying my hardest to find the right way,
but I'm still fighting the fear that is keeping me here.
So, fast-forward four years and I'm standing on stage for the
    first time about to tell my first rhyme,
as I take the mic in hand I feel the blood rush to my face at such
    a rapid pace
and without haste my cheeks go from pale to pink with one
    single wink;
so, I blink, and let myself sink back into me, and not the sea of
    faces staring back at me,
not knowing what to expect as I begin to project.
Then, one minute in and it feels like there's fire underneath my
    skin,
like there's something awakening within,
like my whole life is only just about to begin.
Now I'm turning my curses into verses at the flick of a page,
see, I have learnt a lot for my young age but it's still taken me so
    long to step onto that stage.
But I have broken the fear now,
just to be standing right here now,
and it all seems clear now.
See, fear is just a state of mind
we have to take that risk to see what we can find.

SIMON MOLE

Simon Mole is the poet from the pub, that rapper from the beach, the friendly guy with the big eyes who told that story. His infectious enthusiasm for seeing and re-seeing the world around him is an open invitation for you to do the same. Simon is part of the Chill Pill Collective and Keats House Poets' Forum.

FIXING IT WITH CHEWING GUM
(A Poem To My Granddad)

I close my eyes, and fly with you;
in the Warwick of 293 squadron.
Your living room has the softest chairs
and as we enter the gulf of Trieste
with a four strong Mustang escort,
I lean my head back on the white cotton
of the cushion cover,
and add my own sound-track of soaring strings
and rolling timpani drums. It is 1945,
so the world is a faded chocolate brown,
you are yet to meet Grandma,
and the yanks have arrived,
all fancy kit and wireless operators
who fly with spare transistor sets.
When your's break,
you fix them up with chewing gum.

In the harbour below us
a downed Air-force Lieutenant
waits in a dinghy, under heavy fire from the coast.
We swoop a little lower, banking suddenly above our man
and the airborne lifeboat,
carried under the fuselage of the aircraft,
floats awkwardly down towards him,
parachutes slowing its descent.

The boat lands with a splash,
bobbing half under before righting itself,
as a second round of bullets
tear a trail of fleeting plumes through the waves.
We watch from above as he clambers aboard,
starts up the engine, wheels her around,
and throws up a two fingered V for victory
as he speeds out of the bay.

"Sometimes I wonder what it was all for, was it worth it?"

My eyes open.
The air is grey.
I know it doesn't sound right,
but the air *is* grey.
That point as afternoon meets evening
when maybe the lights should be on,
but nobody has flicked the switch.

And I know,
Without hearing you say it,
that the worth of moments like that
is not what you are questioning.
So, at first I say nothing.

You straighten your tie,
pick up the remote,
and turn the volume up on the telly.

Somewhere, long ago,
the thick smoke of steamships
charts harsh triumph around a stone globe,
and the sun never sets on Britannia's trident.
I see the glint in your eye, or at least its memory,
proud as a whistling kettle.
You have outlived the England you fought for
and yes, you are a brave man, and a kind man
who has done Yoga every day for years,
and in Algiers that time in 43,

it was you who jumped out of the truck
on the way back to barracks
and stopped the drunken white South African airmen
from beating on their black aircrew.
But now, now, there are women in the fire-brigade,
and too many players in the Arsenal team
with names you can't pronounce.
The TV is so loud
and you have taken out your hearing aids
I have to almost shout –
"What about Jack Wilshere, and Walcott,
Theo Walcott!
Wilshere and Walcott: they're English!"
And even though I know that's not the point,
I feel better.

Of course it was worth it,
otherwise Hitler would have won and they were the baddies
and, unlike the history I was taught at school,
you fought in the war simply
to kill as many Germans as you could,
because they dropped the bomb
that nearly killed your old mother.
And I have never said:
there's too many arms in that coffin,
after clearing up the mess on the runway.
And of course I didn't know that, at times like that,
no matter how separate or squashed things are,
most often you find the heads whole.

And it is different now,
less red telephone boxes,
more Polish delicatessens.
At the Festival of Britain, in 1951,
they had a tent called 'The Lion and the Unicorn' –
these two together, our national character,
and I'm courageous with a fierce imagination,
so I want you to know, some things stay the same,
but this England,

which you see as eaten whole by greedy change,
is the only England I've ever existed in.
And yes, there's still fish and chips
wrapped in newspaper wet where the vinegar drips,
just that some of them little wooden chip forks are gripped
by third generation Pakistanis or West Indians, grinning kids,
practicing their bouncers on the village cricket pitch.
Yes there's still Kiss-Me-Quick hats and rainy picnic trips.
Just, alongside cheese sarnies picnic baskets got jerk chicken in,
got that good curried goat, or roti wraps that fingers lift as lips
        are licked.
A million different spices in the air at Brick Lane, mingling
within the nostrils of a couple hungry footie fans in England
        kits.

And I never thought to judge the mixing in, it simply is,
but if I stop to judge it now,
it makes me so proud that you fought and beat the Nazis.
Shit, I'd pull an endless stream of union jack bunting out my
        sleeve
just so we could watch it flutter in the breeze
if I could be sure it would be taken as intended.
Instead I stick with classic English etiquette
Deciding that it's something I won't mention.
"Another cup of tea Granddad?"
"Yes," you say,
"Yes, another cup of tea."

REBEL REBEL

My Dad's Dad had a full-time job as a milkman at fourteen.
Still in short trousers, supporting the family.

Y'know, the get on with it and don't moan generation,
the fought in the war before they could vote generation,
the 'a woman's place is in the home', 'ooh hasn't he grown'
        generation.

Granddad: Telegraph reading one woman man, Conservative
        (big C), proud officer of the London Fire Brigade, brass
        buttons shining, shirtsleeves rolled up.
My Dad, rebelled against all of that.
He was reading Marx before he could walk,
dreaming of leaving fast,
heart suffocated by staunch traditionalism.

The thing is, it's difficult living as an 'Agent of the Revolution'
when you still rely on your father to clothe and feed you.
And certain bonds are broken between you,
then, now and after, when that same father
is most definitely against those 'commie bastards
holding the country to ransom'.

It's 72. And at 18, Dad's gone. Freedom.
But one term of academia later,
the International Socialists have got him selling papers
to the miners up in Scotland 'cause they're striking,
and Dad's wet behind the ears, fresh faced but right beside 'em.

Dad: tarot reading free-love advocate, Trotskyist (big T), proud
        squatter of the London boroughs, shoulder length
curly hair, skinny pretty-boy face, all cheekbones and button
        bright wide eyes shining, fat spliff rolled up.

He went on demonstrations
fist fighting with the Police.
And slept around, when sleeping around
was still considered a politically charged transgressive act.
And as I grew up I heard about it all:

CND activists on acid trips. Anarchists grabbing bricks smashing
shit. Tories closing pits, Socialists groping tits. Passionate
pacifists, arms raised, as 'Ban-The-Bomb' banners lift.
Soundsystems, massive big. Kwesi Johnson, Johhny Rotten,
God save Jagger's lips. Lacking grip. Managing. Tantric mantras
of tie dye tranquility. Happiness. Beads and bandanas, vanishing

dreams and brightly coloured flowers, hands moving freely,
smooth and easy.

And I heard it all in a voice that seemed to say:
"you too can be me"
and most lads look up to their Dads. So there I was, aged seven,
with my home-made hand drawn 'Save The Snails' placard
chanting from the balcony as Dad walked out to the allotment
with a bag of salt, ready to commit murder.

Me: Beano reading Mummy's boy, her anti-authoritarian angel
(three A's), proud son of alternative parents, chin length
Kurt Cobain curtains and Nirvana t-shirt, wide smile shining on
primary school non-uniform day with Mum's culottes rolled up ,
just to prove that 'boys can wear skirts too!'

As for Mum and Dad, needless to say, they loved it.

This was what they had longed for,
in the same way Granddad had wanted Dad
to settle down early to a steady job, wife and kids.

So it's: "Hi I'm Andy's son, Simon,
a thorough-bred, born and well-raised rebel."

Of sorts.

'Cause of course, every rebel needs a cause,
just as every uprising must face a tyrant or evil force.
But teen life is leaving me feeling bored, because
true rebellion needs something to rebel against,
and well, instead, my life's good
and my parents make sure that I get support.
Not to say that it was all plain sailing and never fraught,
and that there weren't storms to weather or father to son talks,
but Dad's sternest words were:
"naughty boy, smoking weed,
and getting caught".

So, though I was raised on tales of the mega-war
Scargill and Maggie waged in the year of my birth, and
reared with a firm and full 'Fuck The Establishment' attitude,
equipped to take the battle to 'The Man',
as a teenager the most important man
to rebel against is your Dad, and
the only option left open to me
was to conform.

I got three A's in my A-levels.
I went straight to Uni, studied hard,
spent more time in the library than the student bar.
And I would love to say that in the family home,
they speak about this in hushed, ashamed tones
like they do about the fact I've never been arrested.

But the truth is, though they had wanted me to rebel,
ultimately they were parents so they loved it when I did well.

Me: Guardian reading graduate committed to long term
girlfriend, academic (capital A plus), proud member of Amnesty
and Friends Of The Earth, hiding my global guilt behind four
pounds a month and neatly trimmed respectable hair, clean
shaven, shining First Class Honours Degree tied with a bow and
rolled up.

TALIA RANDALL

Talia is an artist who likes to write about herself. She plays with Spoken Word and Visual Art because she can't help looking for meaning, even if there isn't any. Talia lives amid continual existential crises and contemplation of what it means to be an artist, so you'll probably find her poking around a fast food shop, trying to make a participative installation out of chicken bones. Talia has performed Spoken Word, and designed activities and installations at venues and festivals across the UK including The South Bank Centre, The Roundhouse, The British Museum and the Edinburgh Fringe Festival. She has also performed in New York.

CHAT UP LINE HAIKU

If female ferrets
don't fornicate when on heat,
they die. It's a fact.

STANMORE

Stanmore fills me with an irrational fear. Every time I'm on the Jubilee line, late at night, heading home I'm scared I'll fall asleep and end up there. I'll be stuck at the end of the line, paying £100 for a cab back to Kilburn.

I've been to Stanmore once and it is mostly Jewish. Full of friendly suburban Ashkenazi's buying houses, marrying young, getting good jobs and visiting their mum's on Fridays.

Jewish places make me feel uncomfortable. They make me feel as if I'm not being Jewish enough. And if I'm not Jewish enough then I don't defend my people and if I don't defend my people then all that suffering could happen again. I can feel this gristly lump lurking just beneath the surface: it's called Jewish Guilt.

Suburban places also make me uncomfortable. Whilst housewives and estate agents see spacious reception rooms, ideal for dinner parties and coffee mornings, I see the hell of Avon ladies: Satan's secret demons sent to Earth to destroy us with fuchsia lipstick and cellulite cream. Whilst some see safe neighbourhoods I see necrophiliacs twitching behind the linen curtains, last year's girlfriend stinking out their cupboards.

I don't like these places because I don't know these places. They are alien to me; they are not in my genetic memory. Because I come from a lineage of working people who thought they were too good for work. People who lived in small houses filled with unwanted marriages and pet budgies.

This was my Dad's upbringing. To me it used to seem awfully romantic; the stuff of black and white films shown on BBC2 at 3am, starring long forgotten heart throbs. Truth is it was probably hellish. A family of 4 living in an asbestos house, made in a factory, built in a day.

But at least Dad had his own room. At his cousin's they all shared rooms. No bathroom. It was worse during their cat phase. Dad told me at one point his cousin had 26 cats in their house. Can you imagine? The floors were crawling, he said. The smallness of their houses squashed the confidence out of these people, until one day, their ambition was crushed too.

And Mum's family. Who could have been wealthy but their communist ideals wouldn't allow it. To the disappointment of his parents my grandfather 'wasted' his training as a lawyer in his job as the editor of a small communist newspaper.

In between covert community meetings and making the children's packed lunch he and my grandmother would run out into the night splashing up communist slogans on the walls of the neighbourhood. "Workers of the World. Unite!" read their homemade posters. This was their attempt to inspire the proletariat of 1950's Israel.

Mum told me how heartbroken they were when they found out what Stalin had really been doing: all those millions. It was more loss than what had come before: in that unmentionable atrocity. In 1956 they took down Stalin's picture from the living room wall and wept.

I remember my grandmother weeping again in front of the news decades later. Shaken by images of tanks smashing through Ramallah. She could have done more, she thought. But her posters couldn't stop the Israeli government ram raiding towards to political right, shedding communist members of the Knesset like lice. Her posters didn't stop those mislead bastards from blowing themselves up. Leaving unrecognisable chunks of flesh along the Tel-Aviv pavements. My grandmother also cried because she missed her husband, and the opportunities they lost because they were denied the pleasure of growing old together. It must hurt to be ideological. It must hurt to be old.

I don't like Jewish places, and I don't like suburban places, but my parents have raised me well. I grew up in a council house, but I had middle class things: singing lessons, foreign holidays, university and an unfair advantage. It therefore seems inevitable that suburbia should form a part of my middle class destiny: a future of mortgage repayments and dinner parties awaits me.

In that future I imagine that there is something else I can't escape. Jewish Guilt will finally get me. That lump will erupt from beneath the surface and claim me: I'll be forced to be as Jewish as I can be to atone for the sins of my youth.

There I'll be, frying latke and getting fat in Stanmore. I'll be stuck at the end of the line, wishing I'd have stayed awake instead of dozing off on the tube, on my way back to Kilburn.

THE DUST

The land is tired.
Worn down by men who claimed the earth for their own.
As centuries turned, conflict became sedimentary.
Rivers were poisoned when water filtered through.
Staining our lips when we drink.

The land dissolves to dust,
blowing in through open windows,
becomes embedded in our pores.
Each particle carries a syllable,
so now we sweat sentences as old as soil.

I'm struggling to comprehend.

The dust is only
half of me.
My other half
is born from England's mountain green.
I'm split down the middle,
each word is like an axe that divides the different sides of me.

The foreign half of me tries.
She absorbs the ancient alphabet
like kitchen towel,
but sounds spill over and I disintegrate.

I have no claim on that biblical territory,
milk and honey can't nourish me enough to speak.
On that land I sleepwalk through conversations,
rocks crumble beneath my feet
no building blocks to lay foundations.
What's left when truth can't transcend translation?
Nothing but waste in a slagheap.

With red English bricks
I can't construct meaning either.
One dyslexic half is too weak to carry the weight of concrete.
and it's not for lack of vocabulary,
English is a bounty

on which I feed.
It's just that, your truth and mine can't meet.
You know what I mean?

I talk but
meaning is bound and gagged,
held hostage in the space
between my lips and brain.

Lost on the journey from my
heart to
my head to
my mouth
to your ear. It

f
r
a g
m
e nt
s

blowing in through open windows.

AMY MCALLISTER

Amy McAllister is an Irish poet living in London. She has been published in South Bank Poetry 8 and also in their special anniversary edition. Amy has won numerous poetry slams around the UK and in Berlin including Farrago, Hammer & Tongue, and the Prop Slam, and was the winner of the Farrago Zoo Award for Best Feature Debut of 2012. Her work was featured in the exhibition Snoring in the USA at NGBK Gallery, Berlin. She has performed live on NTS Radio as a guest on the Re:Versed show, and recently completed a residency at Bang Said the Gun. Amy is also an actress and has appeared in Call the Midwife (BBC), Holby City (BBC), Doctors (BBC), and Emmerdale (ITV).

CROCKERY WORTH WAITING FOR

We blink in our neighbourly darkness like moles,
And debrief the daytime, and search our green souls,
And sleep-break 'appropriate flatmatey roles'.
Then mumble good morning from unmatching bowls.

I choose when to surface and nip to the loo
So we'll meet on the landing, I know you do too.
And you're ever the gent so it's me before you,
Although sometimes that means I've to hold in a poo.

And visitors tell us our banter is bitchin' –
Our comedy show, broadcast live from the kitchen.
And when I feel lonely 'cause London's too big,
You sing Hanson or Backstreet Boys, wearing that wig!

But lately I'm swamped, and you're out having fun.
You've stopped eating pasties and started to run.
You're gone every weekend. You've cut off your hair.
And when I feel down you don't notice or care.

Your tales of the girl you just met from Bermuda
Get ruder and ruder or as you'd say, 'ruduh'.
And I act all Bunny! but feel Barracuda.
'That's so sweet and funny, it's transformed my mood.' Ha!

It couldn't be worse, I can hear you two shagging,
While *my* sex life's tragically, blatantly lagging.

But deep down I know it's a matter of time
'Til I floor you with wit or a Hanson-esque rhyme.
She'll be gone in an mmmbop. You'll soon see the light,
And we'll say 'morning love' over Habitat White.

FESTIVAL, SOBERING

*(Antony& the Johnsons sang with a full orchestra at Wilderness
Festival 2011)*

Crying in a field into the backs of strangers
with only the kindness of the tall Hibernian man
who let me stand in front for a better view.
And all I see and smell and want is you.
I learn from the singing man-lady
that the bits that rotted off will soon grow back.
And I recall my conversation about vegetables with Jack
and how the simple things might make me happy after all
but then I fall again
as cellos keen and heckling voices crack. I fall right back.
And I'm a sicko that's for sure because I love it here,
a mess before this queer and awesome channel of humanity.
I touch my hair to check it's still affected by the laws of gravity
because my feet feel plugged right in to some
grass-covered switchboard of the people –
we're the lightning bolts of love, rejection, family stuff, and fear
and we're all *here*.
And there's a heap of cow and sheep shit but no bullshit,
this is it.
The very human race

with tears and fake moustaches dripping down
our big collective face.
I'm low as lava when it's waiting, and I guess I'm waiting too.
I'm flames and smoke and sulphur
and I'm dormant without you.
But not alone. Hey, this strange creature from some corner
of a culture I don't know sings just how these things go
and there's a couple, rather old and pretty fleecy
to my right who,
in their underhanded stroking, tell me much of their experience
this mind-destroying spirit-saving night. They'll be alright.
And so will I.
Because the tease and swift retraction of real love
has made us all at some point *really want to die.*
Yet this magician has blown silver with his music
through the black holes in the sky.

TRAVELLING

I hope you get that job you went for.
And I hope your road trip's awesome.
And I hope you endeavour to eat most days.
And I hope you make sensible music choices
so as not to tip yourself over on the bad days.
And I hope you remember that the rain is for the grass
and not for *pissing on the embers of your dreams.*
I hope the desert leaves you overwhelmed but in a good way.
And I hope the losses in Las Vegas push the blood into your feet.
I hope the Rocky Mountains numb your bruising with their sleet.
I hope you flirt with girls who are
attractive in their special, one-toothed way,
and that some pretty ones desire you,
and that the feeling that you've lost
your manly instincts goes away.
I hope you learn to ride a horse, because you really wanted to.
And I hope you take forbidden routes because it's what a
German wouldn't do.

I hope glass memories leave you, swept away by earth and wood
and that you see that you can rule the world,
I've always known you could.
I hope Niagara falls on smiling cheeks and open hands.
And I hope you dare to taste the meat from
dodgy hot-dog stands
and wake up six hours later with horrendous swollen glands
so you experience the healthcare systems of these foreign lands.
I hope the subway's creepy and the train is running late,
and the busker on your platform is ridiculously great,
and that you walk when it says don't.
And that you're asked to model for a Benetton commercial
but you won't
because you're busy having pancakes with some dude who used
to set up the equipment for Thin Lizzy.
I hope you feel the sun again
and smell the salt before you see the sea.
And think most mornings of yourself and how you're brilliant
and discover that you are in fact retrievable, resilient.
And I hope your quest for solace leads you one day back to me.

ZARU JONSON

Zaru Jonson has been spouting abstract lit-hop and performance poetry at every opportunity since winning second prize and the audience vote at Literature Wales' John Tripp Award in November 2009. This led to readings at Jam Bones, The Absurd, POETica, Word Life, Cheltenham Poetry Festival, the Dinefwr Literature Festival, the Edinburgh Free Fringe, and a host of other events – largely clustered around Cardiff where he recently completed a degree in English and Creative Writing at Cardiff Met. Chief concerns include God, girls, getting confused between the two, the rejection of everything which constitutes Ginsberg's Moloch, and the coming resurgence of the vibe of the sixties, in which hip-hop hits the hippies.

THE ZARU AS IT STANDS

i am *I W A Z A R U* ;

i am grown from god's stem cells and am slowly becoming aware.

i chew gum.

i would not go opposable
if it meant prosthetic screws for thumbs:

i am he who is dumb
in the knowledge his tongue
will only breed malfunctions

i buy fried chicken
at Llandudno Junction
& cannot see any dead birds, because
i am only prone to symbolist crises
in certain situations.

i cannot sit patiently if there is too much drone in the air at train
                    stations.
on occasion i am left alone in rooms of horrific puce
& can find no other explanation but an immaterial devil.

i have read of Robert Neville.

i am convinced that the world is running on treble
and has disassociated itself from primordial bass
& yea, the soup will vibrate out no first lizard Adam
from all this totally spectral crack and abject whistle squoo –

i am uncertain what to make of the compunctions of my
                    instincts to squeeze thistles
with hands bluemottled from the cold all the August bluebottles
                    told me would come –

i inhabit summer and winter –

lambs and brown leaves mean nothing to me!

like a fifty fifty chance i have a head and a tail.

i am scared to fail!

though by nature androgynous,

in this way i am male.

i have tanned from Maypril onwards
& now i am drawn to things paler than me
like the moon or the memory of Decembuary
when stalebread fed impossible ducks,

a sucker for juxtaposition
seeing it everywhere –

comparing these experiences
with those of my friends,

the contrast of women and men
sends me into crumbledown paroxysms

& i have cataclysmic visions about celestial objects,
dreams which only become sexually symbolic when spoken out
        loud;
delusions that something has broken out now
from a Space Odyssey pandora slab
& crawls crabwise along psychic beaches
reaching into the head of Darwin Turton
who falls, elated, to his knees

into the heads of a hundred others who have stood blatantly at
        ease
with shirts pressed to their chests by this
undeniably ridiculous
wind of a fashion for
deep sea diver helmets
on sunny days –

i pray.

i eat eggs some mornings
and spend some nights on MDMA.

dig the *potential* in spectrumfields of grey
but detest the charcoal soul of the tone of today,
as you can read by whichever facepaints
you last saw me wearing.

i will become extremely vocal on this point
once i get my bearings.

PAINTBRUSH

"my PAINTbrush AIN'T
  crushed nobody's soul"
he said;
banglehand
banginonna
dustbin lid;

  "my PAINTbrush AIN'T
  crushed nobody's soul,
  my PAINTbrush
  just shows
  what *did*."

it was the naked Foot of God.

it was the *discord* after the *sun* went down,
the purple whalesong of our x-ray machines,
all the things that seem to *wipe* the sum homid
mind of the area, & cause small mammals
to anvil out of their trees
from the psychic BOOGIE
of the *ASTRAL PLANE!*

it was *barrels* & *Niagra*.
seeing Christ 'pon the cross,
geese getting shot;
all the things that left INKBLOTS
on your understanding of beauty,
a GIANT SQUID on WHITE SAND – !

(he raised his right hand –
  blocking out the moon with his dustbin lid
  the closest thing he had to a satellite dish

& waiting for whatever messages might come)

"my PAINTbrush
  AIN'T crushed
  nobody's soul,"

he said; his eyes
milky; mad;

"my PAINTbrush
 AIN'T crushed
 nobody's soul,
 my PAINTbrush just shows what *has*."

TRAIN

TRAIN
CRATE
FAULT ON THE SLEEPERS
STEAM
SNAKE
COMBUSTIONCREATURE

O, train,
you and me are the same –
stuck: *here In Hereford!*
with a girl's voice gliding
in both of our heads.

train,
you stay on this side of a yellow line
painted by a hand like mine . . .
you groan on your axis
& your century, & your intercom
speaks with a soul that rhymes
with what the soul of the girl on my mind
meant to me.

but she warns us to WATCH OUT
for anything suspicious . . .
bags of BOOM,

pernicious,
reprobates,
don't we drive you loco?
will the ice slow you down
when i'm dreaming of cocoa ?

train – bear – are we the lice that you fear?
do elephants dream they have mice in their ears?

TRAIN / CRATE / BEAR / NELLY
have your chugalug chugalug feet turned to jelly?

Here in Hereford

where you sit with a panic attack in the pipeline
and wait for me to blow you to kingdom crime?
big slug, we are *brothers*! i fear   like you fear!
i share my room with suspicion and a bag of boom!
and when i wake up, he wakes up
from dreams like mine, of
dissolving floors and pregnancies
and we groan on our axis & our century.

EISH,   CHATANUGA!

the roast duck of my home is far from here
& the night's bowl is cold with no dreg of a rabbit,
we are stuck, because we are both stoned with fear
take control of your faculties,   dammit,

LEST I MAROON MYSELF   *Here in Hereford*
FOREVER!

what is there to *phobe* you in the blanche and madness of Ludlow
before you in all of its darkness dotted with security lights?

GO, GRIZZLY, cleave the night with your sighs
CAREEN LIKE INVENTION in Stevenson's eyes!

the destroyers of bridges wait for you! bandits squat with baited
        breath,
the smoke of their mouths caught in surgical scarves, crate of
        bravery!

run on to Rockbuckle!

dash your face on the unforeseeable hospitalisations
of the future! there will be bicycles thrown on the tracks
and ducks will cross in an exploding somnambula
of FEATHERS, RED FRIGHT, & ambulance tyres!
may gurneys rattle in your wake!
JOURNEY like the patron saint
of tightrope walkers!

ON like the first words of the Beat!
YOU whose romance has dwindled!
may you hurtle
with my blessing like a fuck in the open
and SKIRT on the BRINKS,
ice*skates* hurt *feet*
& the rinks will be *full*,
& your blinks will be mulled
& weary!
go bleary-eyed and tearful
like a seven year old in a chaff-grenade flurry of *sleet*!
hurry, i have people to meet!

go like half-drunk Jesus to a thousand Gethsemanes
and submit to the tender kiss of *whatever*,
FLY! EAGLE! the rockabye beagles of your past

will drop off along the way
and leave you cutting like a *fin*
thru the ball-ache that blows on the wind.

any suitcase might be stitched up to Nitro.
carrier bags will be full of smokey bacon
crisps and bombs

and you will run!

TRAIN, I AM WITH YOU
Here in Hereford
to Ludlow; from Marathon
from Athens to Avalon
ready to die screaming "NENIKIKAMEN"

with a question mark dithering above my head
like an angel in the crash position,
ready for our collision
and the mild concussions
of eternity,

safe in the dire straits of
my own sweet maudlin little woolscrunch of
dangerous human life & Baloo,

TRAIN – CRATE – ME&YOU -
CHUG, BIG SLUG,CHATANUGA,

whooh whooh

DEANNA RODGER

Deanna Rodger is a member of London poetry collectives Chill Pill, Come Rhyme With Me, Rubix, Keats House Poets' Forum and Point Blank Poets. She was the youngest UK Poetry Slam Champion (2008), and has performed her poetry at Buckingham Palace, Number 10 Downing Street, Speakers House and many other prestigious venues, theatres and events around the UK. Deanna wrote the Olympic Team Welcome Ceremony and is an actor. Deanna cites her influences as 'being alive, living in a world filled with other people and by having a brain that works'.

22NOW

See red, sprint and pounce on to the now novelty open back
      Routemaster,
Out of breath from the effort,
Spiral up steps and seat search for the backseat of the top deck.
Breathe in the musky scent
And lean into a time where 3D TV's are only seen in sci-fi
      fantasies,
And you know no smart phone
So this bus journey isn't spent alone with app games and emails
Your oyster exists as an unexplored world
Notebook opened in your lap is a pearl
Polished by prophesied arrival of school girl gabble, loud and
Charged by coppers that skip in pockets when your valentine
      red bus runs past a PG common hesitant to stop.

You watch our chase.
Seduced by the vulnerabilities of the open air bus,
We stride towards the choice of extra curricular adventure,
Stretching skirted legs, as far as they can go,
Before leaping and
Chanting at friends that lack the co-ordination of limbs

Loyal, you see us hang off poles holding the driver's stare with
        spider like lashes until all legs are aboard
the two two Piccadilly bound bus.

Once we are up, you relish the clarity of our educated insults
        over the best,
Small enough for one, big enough for two, back of the bus bench
        like toothless scavengers,
Tongues sharpening at each step,
Breath deepening with a rubber like resistance,
Pulse fuelled adrenaline loading
Like arrows
Taunt to release
As your own breath is held to exhale, we do so passively at sight
        of you through brace straight teeth.

We move in a cloud of impulse
Wearing inside out blazers,
Because we are fresh princesses free from an all lady posh
        school,
To hang off second choice seats in sport chic converse low cuts,
        an urban amendment of our boat friend's high laces-
        tied-to-the top converse geek-ness.

She had the foresight we pretended to see through slick hair and
        lip-gloss.

She plugs in with two working Christmas white earphones
Orchestrating songs from Monica's *After The Storm* album
Our shallow notes conducted by a mismatched,
Not yet retro Walkman that stretches a scarred girl's pocket
Bangs against her hip and skips the semi scratched CD on our
        bouncing straight road journey.

Traffic exhausts our patience; the button to leave is pushed
Ejecting us and you follow
To speed down staircase narrow and steep and join us in our
        bus hop off 22s to search for 19s
Paper passes are expertly fake, made in Math class with the skill
        only trial and error can create

But we don't wait at bus stops; we stroll with urban limps down
        Kings road
Bus watching
Clocking salacious backseat boys
Ready to jump on to taste scents of the top saloon and jump off
For chase from the after-shaved adolescents.

Sloane square drowns post bus ruckus and saturates our strolls
        to stops
To watch people criss-crossing every crack of space
Like water
Grey suits
Trickle through
Barriers
We are shy of
Electric shutters look
Aggressive and unforgiving
And map of string strangles our numbers
With order and law so we stay away
Curiously watching

As you beep in, thinking about
Scenes set under the eye-lidded windows that oversee paired
        seats of no separation, like the updated CCTV and
                stickers safe, yet to be peeled like scabs on
                        schoolboys knees.
You leave these young inquisitive ladies on land level not yet
        ready to explore
The underworld, for in that time where cycling wasn't a trend
        yet and there are no narrow pathways painted onto the
                road
They are safe knowing that if they ever fall in their leaps of faith
They will laugh through the pain
Because it is all you can do when trying to
Master the route.

LOVE WITH TIME

'I love you'
Mind maximises effects of words I've heard escape from a
          mouth borrowed and placed on my face
Cos I've
Felt this feeling before,
Of more,
More time, touch, texts,
Affectionate attention
Too much is not enough
But
It was lust
Pure, lust.

I'd lost sense and jumped into the endorphin mix
Where courage and confidence were clumped together, pumped
          with Cupid's drug and labelled love.
To me it was lovely.
But he, was immune
And refused to consume from pit where boils would burst
Releasing statements that slipped out as easily as he
Slipped in.
So,
'I love you'
Brings me to when once silence answered back initially,
          immediately
Replaced by a 'me too' bear hug.
I thought bared words
Worth more
Than the cliché I'd sold for free.

'I love you'
Drums pick up beat
Of a heart
That's destined to be
Torn apart
By a girl who's yet
To be hurled from past
Into present.
A gift patiently waiting for the

Stubborn child who threw tantrums at parents
Just in need of reassurance
That
Mother's insurance was for life
Not on loan
Nor a replacement for a broken phone
Or a Trocodera token
To be
Traded in for the real win.

What am I thinking?
As legs sink in to a hypochondriac's chair,
I'm scared
So tough to 'I love you too'
Let me flicker eyes with care, prepare the
'Me too'
Echoed reply of what I received so long ago,
Knowing it'll
Resound as it rebounds in his mind
I'm compulsively being kind
By cushioning with foam squares,
Reused, resilient
Right angled truths

As I return, to my 8 crumpled letters,
Wondering whether
'I still' was really 'I never'
As our relationship was as rocky as the caramel chocolate bars
        our skin colours matched.
And 'do' is 'really did'
Cos he did do the do
Digging deep inside a womb
To miscarriage mans ignorance which once grasped the sharp
        parts of a one way mirror,
Deceiving me to believe that the reflection of just one was
        actually two

Now I see only you.
Phantasmal to me

But yet you pursue to fine tune a
Facsimile of my own broken record

You say 'I love you'
I say $1 + 4 - 3 = 2$

SOMEONE LIKE WHO

Someone like who?
Someone like he, her or you?
You with no backbone,
Stupid bitch follow ball when it's thrown
Retrieve to take back,
Conditioned by the master,
What?
Someone like that?
Within the BMI but with a bull mental image of fat
Girls chat,
Call chubs,
So she
Empties
Stomach of a B and J tub.
Blub or blob?
Active as ADH but with a belly of a slob.
Sob.
Poor little thing,
She just wants to be thin
Attractive to all
Lusted after by him.
See he
Left she
In the park cos he caught a sudden whim,
Whiff of her,
Her sweet scent aroused a purr.
So he whisked her away,
While she
Strayed,

Played,
Betrayed,
Made bed before she laid,
Down and dreamt of becoming a
Gang-banger
A hard nut
A crazy girl
With hard luck
Hustle life
Ambitions rife
When road calls she goes to buck.
In the cycle washed to clean
Stripped away legitimate dreams
To achieve the goal she steals the means
In regards to men she keeps 'em keen
Treats 'em mean,
So they fiend
Keep her preened
While she gets lean
Leans back and thinks
It could all be over in a blink
Though amour holds no kinks
She's aware that, at, any single wink she'll sink
Be brought to the brink where inner strength shrinks
With ego
Though minds impenetrable as a bullet proof vest
She still settled for less
Caved into contest
Couldn't compete with a milk-coloured breast.
So,
She gives it a rest.
But betrayals bruises still show,
White like the image of snow
On clichéd Christmas cards
Her, body knows not of what the mind has barred
Scarred perception
Processed to deception of what's normal
Moon falls,
She wakes,

Takes, just a second hour to teleport to shower and white wash,
        not shed but paste over undesirable skin colour.
Hunchback so bum's flat,
Straighten fro then backcomb
Transition to someone who needs not a uni loan.

Unlike the other sister,
So-called fussy one.
Middle of three but
Joint first for mum
Drunk share so she
Thirsts for more
Hydrate mind man-kind can't afford to ignore.
She writes rhymes on her hand.
Ink-prints new land,
Of a destiny that demands she see palm trees
From a shepherd's dream,
Pyramids and faithless thieves,
To find only what's found if she truly believes
That someone like she
Will someday be,
Someone like me.

PAUL CREE

Paul is a writer and performer from Horley in Surrey, now based in London. His background is rooted in music, having come from a family of musicians and beginning his foray into writing lyrics as a MC and a rapper. He has since gone on to write poetry and short stories and performs regularly both as a spoken word artist and in theatre productions. He is currently a member of the Rubix Collective. He's one of seven children and occupies the rare and precious Rhesus Negative blood group.

THE 21.00 TO NOWHERE

One of several
large flat screen TV's blink silently.
Rotating an incessant stream of updating information
from the world of football
and a few other sports,
which fight like pigeons over the remaining crumbs of coverage.
Muted to a theme tune of songs
played over the PA
belonging to a decade before.
Lip syncing Sky Sports news readers
with Snow Patrol or Oasis becomes a game in itself.

The many human pillars of unofficial knowledge
that often populate pubs,
normally stood like dusty ornaments at the bar,
will tell you the breweries pay less in PRS for the older songs
like it's some grand racket that none of us are supposed to be
        in on.
But this is no normal pub.
This particular establishment,
with its sports screens,
high bar stools and signed shirts in frames
will rarely produce such loyal patrons

due to the nature of the clientèle they serve on a daily basis,
for they belong in train stations.
Suspended animation between places as people revolve
as fast as turnstile gates on packed match days.

Located conveniently between A and B,
these are the types of bars which I never remember the name of,
but chances are
I'll know what beers they sell
and how much they charge,
and I'll quietly tut when I receive my change
on a shiny silver tray with a receipt
including the VAT breakdown and the bar tender's name,
which in this case is Pascal
(not that we're on a first name basis).
It's that lack of familiarity which appeals to me.

With décor and furniture
generic enough
that even the most eccentric amongst us can blend in
and become anonymous.

In here I don't exist.
Trapped between time zones for when I have no place to go.
This soulless sports bar is a waiting room
where I can consult my heart and pick apart my brain
or just simply sit,
sip
and switch off.

I watch as commuters
come and go for a post-work drink.
Some look as if they're buying their time
before the big squeeze back to the provinces.
Tourists browse the expensive food menus
in which oven-heated ready meals appear at the blink of an eye.
Groups of lads and girls break journeys downing booze at
            breakneck speed

before they leave to presumably go on elsewhere to drink even
more.

If I sit here long enough
the merry go round of sports updates
will produce a new piece of news.
I might even hear a song I once liked.
The few pound coins in the tray
the £10 note residue used to pay for a pint
may not even see the dark cotton cushion of my pocket
and may just be popped into the slot
of a fruit machine
depending on how low I sink.

Today I'm sat
three feet off the ground
on this high stool
nursing an expensive pint
poured by Pascal
and I will take my time.
This bar is my camo-pattern jacket hidden amongst the leaves,
and when I'm ready
I'll slowly slip off my stool
and go locate my train.

SHE SAYS

You sit on a cold, hard, shapeless plastic chair
In a sterile hotel corridor
which smells of damp towels
disinfected of life.
Sipping on tasteless tea
bought from an overpriced machine
whilst the love of your life
is in the wedding suite,
sipping on champagne,
making love to a man with bigger muscles

99

but not much to say.
You tell yourself he's alright
and you're happy for her
whilst pretending
you can't hear her high pitched moans,
which fracture
the fine wine glass rim of your feelings
and his
low frequency mumbles
like earthquake tremors
to the very structure of your manhood,
because when she's done
you're giving her a lift home
like you always do,
because you're friends,
she told you so,
and you agreed.

ADAM KAMMERLING

Adam Kammerling is the Hammer And Tongue UK Slam Champion 2012. He has been featured in theatres, venues and pubs all over the South of England and performed at Glastonbury, Latitude, Big Chill and numerous other festivals in the UK. He cut his teeth at the open-mic cyphers and rap battles of the Brighton hip-hop scene. Since 2007 he has been performing his own brand of highly eclectic poetry across the UK and overseas. Weaving numerous voices through his own, he incorporates elements of poetry, rap, theatre and comedy to create immersive, engaging works that push the boundaries of performance poetry. His favourite chocolate bar is the rare and elusive Kinder Maxi.

RETURNING TO THE SEA

I always felt small on Brighton beach.
On dry days off, grey or bright, I'd burrow my bum into stones,
make a clacking niche for a seat
and stare till I shrank to a match head, pink between the
            pebbles.
After five years I was tired.
The sea and I had nothing left to say.
Our new mutedness took root and spread like nettles,
spooned silence on the promenade
and eeked through town to Moulsecombe.
Cafés hushed and clunked, blunt like wood.
Drugs rang like bottle banks all around
and I could never get a seat in a pub.
Waves splashed like house cats now,
abandoned the moon and gagged for paddling.
London mocked.
I thought he was real cool.
I did one.

On a January day, coat-scarf-hatted, leaning into wind,
eyes pinched, gloved hands clasped in Rosy's
I walked the seafront, Hove to Shoreham.
Sun-full in brisk light I took to the wall,
leaping gaps where steps stepped down,
my toddler's mouth jumped with me.
Quickly conversation waned,
in it's place the grumbling tide,
drumming its foamy fingers,
pinkie first then fanning
like a hand of cards or pigeons
swooping one by one, roof to crumbs.
Behind me Brighton yawned,
a voiced deliberate yawn of boredom.
And I would have yawned too,
three years ago.
But the sea cannot bore.
The oldest fidget,
always limber, wrists skip tipping
the ride while toes tap stresses,
brushes skim tom skin, rhythm is held
through all of our dissonant improvisations.
Horizon's gentlest arc speaks of space
and the nub of my mind-span.
Tides swing for infinity.
And I'm a match head again, between the pebbles
and they're rough enough to spark off.
I flex toes in trainers, walk the wall
jumping steps, Hove to Shoreham,
Rosy walks ahead,
the sea rumbles at my side.

WOOFQUACKMEOWNEIGHMOOOINK

His sunken eyes are ringed in grey,
pupils peer from cold flesh caves,
facial hair sprouts like mould,
his casual sportswear's dripped in stains.
Those eyes find a shadow of me
and I wish he'd sit elsewhere.
His questions come rapid fire,
inconsequential, like sonar.

What's your name?
Adam
Where are you going?
Hastings
What are you doing? What are you doing in Hastings?
I'm doing a gig.
What colour is the train?
Uh...
What colour is the carriage?
Blue.
Why is the carriage blue?
I don't know.
Why is the carriage blue?
Maybe neutral colours?
Why is the carriage blue?
Uh...
Why is the carriage blue?

He carries a blind-man's cane
but his better eye flicks as landscape snaps in to the carriage's
          wake.
I fling my own question through the galaxy of his and he replies

In a house near MEOW!

And in the same heartbeat he restarts
his white water inquisition, head twitching all the while
his boss eye wanders, he claps beneath the table
when my answers match his plans.
He mentions Eminem, Harry Potter

And *Could this train bash the other train?*
And *Why do dogs have one head?*
I laugh, and I make him laugh,
a fluffy, globular guffaw.
I hesitate, shamefully,
when he asks my girlfriend's daughter's name
and where she lives and where is that?
He says his name is WoofQuackMeowNeighMooOink
And asks *Is that a long name?*
The instant we pull into Eastbourne
he is at the carriage door,
still rattling questions till he is gone.
No goodbye, no see you,
No good luck, nice to meet you,
just a question, a question, a step
and he is gone.
I find a seat on my Hastings connection,
busy with people, bright with the first flashes of spring
like I'd woken from an uneasy sleep
alone, on a train.

FOX

Bad vibes found the conversation tonight and it never quite
        revved its way back,
I shared an illicit chicken kebab with youngers who spoke only
        ironic slang,
I pissed openly on a road in torrential rain.
Now my left foot is squelching in the big toe area and a fox lies
        dead at the edge of the pavement.
Wet fur makes it fake, like sushi in the windows of sushi shops,
Its last fox-moments; glowing vapour trails in 3am-empty roads,
budding puddles and bright white lines are stern and hard-eyed
        witnesses.
It holds my eyes like a skull. A wasting scar on the calves of the
        night.

I do not nudge it with my rain and piss soaked toe, though the
        little meanness inside me would have it.

A bus is coming but I want to hear this life expired like the last
        slurps of a milkshake,
find purpose or meaning in death, that's what writers do, right?
        And poets?
But death should be a private business, especially for foxes.
I have stumbled drunk, wet-ragged and slow, into a forbidden
        space mid-ritual,
swivel-heads catch my staggers, too late to style this out.
My bus is coming. But who will mourn? Am I mourning now
        and what gives me the right?
Luck? Maybe. My sense of righteous shuts its mouth and lowers
        its eyes, as well it should.
The curved glass-bottom still crackles through the rushing of
        sucking air
but it's raining and my skin sits wetly against clothes' failure
        and my bus is coming.
I throw my arms and marvel at the lack of mess, with a last look
hug the sight to mind, then chase my bus to the bus stop.

ROB AUTON

York born word-sayer Rob Auton has recently become a household name, in his own house at least. He has had his poetry played on the radio by Jarvis Cocker, starred in a film adaptation of his poem *Footballer's Life For Me* on Channel 4, and was recently described by film director Paddy Considine as "a very funny man". Rob also continues to co-run the hugely popular London poetry extravaganza Bang Said the Gun, a poetry night for people who do not necessarily sleep under duvets made entirely from poetry books. He does not like fig rolls.

BACON

Francis Bacon and Kevin Bacon are the rashers from a very
       talented pig
the pig could paint
the pig could act
the pig was a genius as a matter of fact

STARS

The dead crouch down to the floor of heaven each holding a pin. When it's dark enough they prick the paper-thin floor of heaven that doubles as the ceiling to our... thing. This allows a tiny bit of heaven to shine through. It looks bright up there. If it is that bright all the time how does anybody get any sleep? Maybe you don't need sleep. The electricity bill must be huge, having lights on like that all the time.

TARMACCED

Today
The roads were tarmacced
The pavements were tarmacced
The hills were tarmacced
The mountains were tarmacced
The fields were tarmacced
The rivers were drained and then tarmacced
The animals were put to sleep and then tarmacced
The flowers were tarmacced
The paintings were tarmacced
The music was tarmacced
The forests were chopped down and then tarmacced
The clouds were tarmacced
The sky was tarmacced
The moon was tarmacced
The sun was tarmacced

ESCAPE THROUGH THE EYES

I woke in the morning whilst you continued to sleep.
I could see small clusters of sleep had gathered on the end of
          your eye lashes.
As I looked closer they appeared to be tiny heads.
Screaming mouths with scrunched eyes made up pale petrified
          faces that dangled from the ends of your eyelashes like
                    raindrops about to fall from the tips of leaves.

It was as if the nuggets were trying to escape from your head
          through your eyes.
Your nightmare was too much for them to take.

SOCKS

Dark is the palette of my sock drawer,
I open it and bats fly out.
All that's missing is a moon, and a werewolf howling at it.
I could pick a sock at random, tie it around my arm and pay my
        respects to the dead.
My sock puppets are dressed for a funeral,
they cry dark cotton tears,
magpies without the white bits,
humbugs without their stripes,
badgers covered in coal.

GRIM GENIE

I rubbed the golden magic lamp with my palm and the Grim
Reaper appeared in a puff of smoke.
"Oh, I was rather hoping for a Genie" I said.
"I am working as a Genie from today, as I was recently made
        redundant as Death" he said, looking at the ground,
                with his hood covering his face.
"Well I only have one wish and that is to die." I replied.
Death stared me in the face and began to sob.

EMMA WARD

Emma is a proud daughter of the West Country, only just of age and recently out of the whole schooling business. She started performing poetry less than a year ago probably as a result of seeing some great traditional fireside storytellers as a child. Her style could be described as urban, slightly cooler story telling for adults. She likes cycling, cider, tree climbing, Roger Deakin and wild swimming. Emma is influenced spiritually by Native American philosophy but artistically by music, experiences and other people. She is currently saving up the pennies to get out of the city and cure her itchy feet, planning to "woof my way through Europe, preferably to somewhere mountainous with good lakes".

JUNE ON THE WEST COAST

Knee-deep in exam season, the City. Library. Scene.
High windows, higher ceiling and my whole year seems held
in the pressurised hush of a hundred working silently
save the sound of chair scrapes and shuffled sheets,
of the runny-nosed pen-scratched cleared-throats
and one incongruent Londoner I've brought with me,
who shifts, un-concentrated, from hip to hip on his wooden chair.

Over an eye-brow high partition there's rows of the hundred
          foreheads
all nose down or fist to cheek or furrowed brow but then,
sometimes a pair of eyes, like mine, who quickly look away,
whose statistical analysis must be far more dull than forehead
          gaze.
But the Londoner fixes stressed eyes of June to his work,
this man of the capital who holds the weight of a monopoly name
          on his shoulders
London LON-DON saaafeasterrn taaaan
that ferments in lapping waves of individualism, of

multiculturism, the impulse-driven taxi-hailed all night
simmering livelihoods in small spot parties and smoky
        palm-held dreams.
A man who isn't any taller than me if I'm wearing my
        Doc-Martens.

But the afternoon stretched out indoors is lethargic and
            compressed, and condensed to checklist chores and pen-
                tip paralysis.
I stroke the curve of his darkly shaved head
looking naked in the place where his dreadlocks used to be,
and pausing, finger padded, cradle brink of neck
and after eyelid flicks brush lip uncertain lip.
I straighten up again. The library is paralysis,
and I can tell that a couple rows away
some pairs of pupils point towards us,
in the library's hush, in boredom.
I leave.

DEATH RETURNS FROM HIS BANK HOLIDAY WEEKEND – MILK WOOD STYLE

A cloudless sky and one small town, lullabied by whispered
        breeze.
The grass grows, the sun beats and horses sigh,
in baying restlessness they hoof over hoof, continue to graze.
In the yards the chickens peck and scratch
while thick-boned cats droop lazily on cottage walls,
their claws sheathed, eyes shut in cat dreams.
And the whole of this rural-spun, feet on the ground town pauses
and seems to hold its breath as death is re-introduced.

Doctor Dan works at his desk, pensive and elbow-deep in
        medical journals.
He's calculating bedspace and the rate of unemployment in the
        mortuary.

His fingertips tap tap beats on the mountain high pile of paper
        sheets, detailing diagrams of diaphragms and hearts.
And through his window you can see him shifting his head from
        fist to fist, a green vein throbbing snake-like in his
            temple.
And only you can smell the sweat of this one, troubled, country
        doctor
counting the reserves in his woodpile, the potatoes in his cellar,
the farmers coming to him for help because their hay won't
        harvest,
their scythes won't slice and the corn stalks now grow too strong.
He's measuring the droop of laden apple-trees with their never-
        pickable fruit,
the anthills on his lawn and the coma patients who don't know
        they're born.
Their hearts bleep incessantly on their machines in the coma-
        patient ward.

But down the cobbled town track, past the marble playing,
        muddy-kneed children wrapped up in their own spring
            worlds, is preacher Pete in the stone chapel.
"Rejoice!"
His voice echoes the windows, empty seats and the thrice padded
        flagstones under his feet.
"Rejoice! Poverty: cured! Deforestation: abandoned!
Woman and man united to serve God endlessly.
'Til death do us part? No more!
For death is the scurvy of the past,
the knee-knocked, fleeting blind velvet past that was, but now…
For life, for life we do unite!   Oh lord this is the greatest
                spring that ever was."

In his private preaching place where the placid air now dares to
        breathe,
Preacher Pete sighs contented, but then
a little sorrow that he might never smell the sweet scent
of a fresh mown lawn lingering in summer air again.

So Doctor Dan is bureau bound and Pete is too, to holy ground,
when the encroaching death sense of decay returns to the village
        compost heap.

ODE TO THE SUB-PEDESTRIAN MENDIPS

I am the mud of the underground, the unfound hidden rivers and
        trickling streams
trembling in cupped caving fingers – a water rock-rendered sweet
I am the helectite, the unexplained gravity-defied rock formation
tugging at the corners of passers by.
I am the stalactite and stalagmite that wait a billion years to kiss,
that every drip brings closer to it
until they form a pillar for us to knot a rope around
and belay, one-eyed into the darkness.
I am the flow stone, the fossil shrimp
and the eroded floor of long-vacated seas.
I am the perfect foothold, just when needed that makes you think
that caves were made for caving in.

So down in the underground, following the water down, the
        waterfall route inside – now a path well glossed by the
        boiler-suit slide
by the caver who, foot to ceiling and forehead first, fumbles
        Eastwater's upper traverse,
who felt the weight of softened rock against their chest and
        paused,
picturing the village green a mile above
and the whistling villagers' unhindered steps thinking their
        overground thoughts.
Who brooded over cave pearls and painted faces in the gloaming
the short cuts and broad leaps
and hid to scare the too clean Scout groups
down corridors that follow like a strained metaphor
who, with helmet sanctity nose dived into the bear pit
and emerged bruised elbow and shin

but smiling the grubby, wet-nosed smile of adrenaline and
    exploration instinct fulfilled.
Who revelled in the sunless dark, the palm to nose-tip blindness
and mapped out the shape of caverns by the drips in different
    parts
and found peace in the mirrored beats of the heart.

Who surfaced out of Swildon's entrance – in the roots of an old
    stream tree
and put back on their city skin, swung knees under work desks
    restlessly
and counted out the days until their knees were padded, wellied
    and again
back down in the belly of the world.

I am the vertical wanderlust.

RAYMOND ANTROBUS

Raymond Antrobus is a spoken-word poet and photographer,
born and bred in Hackney. He is co-founder of popular spoken
word night Chill Pill and Keats House Poets' Forum. He has
performed alongside authors and poets such as Margret Atwood,
Michael Horovitz, Lemm Sissay, Polarbear and Inua Ellams.
Raymond has been performing spoken word poetry since 2007.
He was the International Farrago slam champion in 2008, Anti-
Slam Champ 2010 and won Best Performance by a London poet
at the Farrago annual poetry awards in 2010. Raymond has
toured internationally, performing in Berlin, Venice, New York,
Cape Town and Chicago. He is a member of the spoken-word
collective known as A Poem inbetween People (or PiP) who have
been described as "London's hottest spoken word talent" by The
Times.

MY VICES – WOMEN & BROKEN POEMS

Norah. Hold my writing hand.
Help me write the things

I can't say to you.

I trust you.
Norah. I sit alone with you.
You brush your fingers
along my tattooed arms,
and ask if I have a condom.
You are smarter than me.

This is the universe where
I would marry my words

if I was sure they were right.

I always feel something is missing
but never know what it is. Norah,
I feel love is a type of clean, and
I'm too dark for it. Too cut up.
If there was a licence for love,
I'd have points for speeding,

so I caution you.

I am not the ride

If you don't want to crash.

I'm a love child, so
everything about me is an accident

or a broken poem

or a good idea that doesn't work.

But if I write about you, Norah

I always try to do it well.

ONE NIGHT AT ZULA BAR IN CAPE TOWN

I'm dancing,
        I'm dancing more
                I'm dancing more than I ever danced,
more than I did at my cousin's wedding,
more than I danced on my 21st Birthday
(which was a 70's roller disco)
                I drink Milk Stout beer
        at the Zula Bar
and dance with girls I won't take home.

I haven't slept in weeks,
but I'm still doing the shuffle with the 3am crowd,
It doesn't matter how much I miss my sister
even though we've never danced in the same room.
Doesn't matter that my dad won't be alive by the time I
      understand him.
Doesn't matter that I might be talking
      to my grandma's grave stone by the time I'm home.
Doesn't matter that my entire family think I'm strange
and I think they are normal.
Doesn't matter that I should have told Sophie the truth,
that I didn't want another person in my life that I could lose or
      let down.
             Doesn't matter that it's 4am now

and behind me a girl is yelling
This music is so good it hurts!

And I'm dancing, dancing like dancing is a kind of pain, and all I
      can do is
          shake.

INTERROGATING DEPRESSION

Before you hit the garden party
consider your mood –

is it a water can
or a bad cloud?

You're doing your best
to feel like the right weather.

You know if it stays too long
you won't look both ways
when crossing the street.

You try to peel it away
like a towel
that wipes your dirt.

It shows in pictures
you don't want taken.

When you talk to it
is your language loud enough
to ask what dark spot
you can meet at?

Will it show up
in a mine cart
as a shadow in a rain coat?

Will it sleep
next to you
and dream your plane crash
into the ocean?

Does it come just to change
the colour of your day?

How much light can you touch inside your
self

Where no one hears
how it hides in laughter
that almost has you dying.

This is why you started running
through the marshes
noticing how grass sags
around the filter bed.

Bicycles understand you
they feel every bump
in the road.

117

They're chained to railings
watching cars move
with speed
they'll never have.

Your weight
keeps you slow
you can't keep up with the keep-coming
mornings.

You see the whole moon
as a creature
that eats you,

it takes the current
out your water
with the skill to drown you
silently
making waves no one rides
but you.

If this is true,

you are not the right weather,

you will not go
to the party.

BRIDGET MINAMORE

Bridget Minamore is a 20-year-old student from South-East London who has written with the National Theatre's New Writers programme, had her poems exhibited at a TEDx London conference and met the Queen at a reception for Young Artists. Writing poetry since she was 17, she has performed at the Roundhouse, 10 Downing Street and the King's College Cambridge Women's Dinner. A member of both Point Blank Poets and Rubix poetry collectives, in 2011 she went to Rome to represent the UK at the Biennial of Young Artists from Europe and the Mediterranean. In 2012 she took part in The Guardian's £100 Challenge out of which came her excellent pamphlet, *The Ice Cream Manifesto*.

KING'S COLLEGE HOSPITAL

Love
is holding your baby girl to your chest
after leaving work early
because she has a fever
and reading her a story
that she simply cannot understand because,
if we're honest,
her brain is the size of a golf ball,
and the information that it holds
revolves around her mother's breasts
and calming her cries so her Mum
can have a rest after being up with her all night
because that is just what you do.

And Love
is waking up
at 12.04 in the morning
and stretching and yawning
and putting on clothes

and driving to A&E because
he came home pissed
and he missed a step
and he thinks he's broken his collarbone, again,
and sitting around watching BBC News
and avoiding the drunks
and needing the loo
but just staying put – just in case – the nurse
calls his name whilst he has a snooze,
and stroking his hair as he tosses and turns
with his head in your lap, until dawn
because that is just what you do.

MELANIE

She doesn't want to be a white girl...
just a little bit lighter.

More Mariah Carey than Oprah Winfrey.
More Halle Berry than Alek Wek.
More Vanessa Williams on Ugly Betty,
than the Williams sisters on Centre Court –

so, she's bought some creams.

"I'm not using anything extreme"
she reassures her friends.
But I'm not one of them,
so I'm unimpressed,
and maybe even a little scared
as she cannot seem to comprehend
why I boo and hiss and take the piss
when I see she bleaches her skin.

Fact is? She looks pink.
And I can't see how she thinks
she looks in any way attractive.

My friends tell me there's a reason behind it,
but I don't understand.
They say "things aren't always black and white"
and in this case I think they're right
as with bleaching skin you'll always find
a hundred shades of pink and orange
scattered in between.
From Michael Jackson
to Michael Jackson,
it's something we've all seen.
If she wants to bleach her skin, they think,
it's all a cover for the bigger picture.
They all have their theories,
but I'm not sure which is right.

Shamarah's sure it's to do with status.
In the way that years ago the way you'd show
that you were rich and never worked outside,
was by hiding from the scorching sun
in a desperate attempt to lighten your skin.
She says it's all to do with colonialism.

I just think that girl looks pink.

Kayela says she's just unhappy.
Chynna thinks it's kind of sad.
And when she comes near Kourtney whispers
"Look at what her skin's become,
it looks sore. Red raw. It's so… bad"

Mia likes to blame the media.
The sexy, seedy, celebrity world
where you're only perfect if you follow
the rules to be famous like everyone else.
A place where female celebrities
like to change the tone of their skin.
Whether with bleach or L'Oreal adverts,
she's sure, the industry is to blame.
The same old story every day

because it's a no win situation.
And Mia says it strikes a nerve
with black girls everywhere –
that it makes us mad because naturally
we can't compare to this Westernised idea of beauty.
And this girl I know is sad enough
to want change her skin.
And I know I should feel bad for her
but I can only focus on the fact this girl looks pink.

Malika says it stems from slavery.
Back in the days when a white man
got his black maid pregnant and
she'd give birth to a light-skinned child.
A girl. A small, tiny baby who'd enter the world
with a father who offered not diamonds and pearls
but disowned her and called her a nigger.
And when she had grown and had got a bit bigger
she worked for her father in the dirt of the plantation,
just like everyone else.
And the men who slaved in the scorching heat
would try to meet the mixed-race girls
who weren't as haggard as the rest
because their fathers – in an act of kindness –
tried to treat them best.
And if you were with the boss's girl
you'd be treated well and whipped much less.

That's why she tries to be lighter, Malika says.
Malika did Psychology at school so, obviously,
she must know what she's talking about –
but if I'm honest, I'm not sure what to say.
I haven't got a proper answer; I just know what I think.

That some girl, in my college, looks pink.

THE CLEAN VERSION OF 'YONKERS'

Things that don't make sense to me:

Long division.
Life.
Poverty.
Boob jobs.
Misery.
People allowed to stay starving and unhappy.
The meteoric rise of Kim Kardashian.
All fashion, in general, especially couture.
Death.
The fact I wept over the movie Armageddon.
The lack of democracy in this country.
People who say sorry all the time, like me.
Things that you once said to me.
Things that don't make sense.

Because we look at each other and it's awkward now.
I was around... You were here. Near. Called.
Said, let's meet here, it'll be easy.
I had to walk past there to get home and you know that.
I said yes. Only because I had to walk there to go home though,
only because it was on the way home though,
only for that reason.
I called again when I saw you. There. Here, with her,
you didn't mention her and this didn't make sense.
So I called you first.
Asked where abouts you were even though I could see you,
I wanted you to warn me but you didn't.
I walked up.
Told you to turn around and smiled like this wasn't a problem.
Like she wasn't, like this wasn't a problem.
I hugged her first. You picked me up like you always do,
always did, and I gripped you tighter than I normally do because
I knew – not much. Just that you and me and us
didn't make sense anymore. You put me down and
said the same questions you never normally ask –
how are you, what's uni like and blah, blah, blah –

I wasn't listening. We spoke some more, I said goodbye and I left. No, backwards glances. No, turning back, then.

Things that don't make sense to me:

Me, seeing you, especially when I know that I shouldn't do.
The stock markets.
Maths.
The wrath some people feel towards celebrities.
You calling him, He, when you know his name and you chose
        this.
Us.
Us keeping us a secret.
Women's marital statuses always being known due to 'Miss' or
        'Mrs' but men just being known as Misters.
Kisses on the cheek from you, to me.
Kisses between us.
The clean version of 'Yonkers'.
Me, whenever I listen to misogynistic rap music.
That time, then.
The ice-cream section in Sainsbury's without any Häagen-Dazs.
The way they used to look at us.
The war in Iraq, and
the fact that you only get sign language on the TV at night, like all
        deaf people are nocturnal.
The fact we might meet up again soon.
Racism, in all its forms.
Sexism, for all its norms.
Page 3.
Katy Perry nominated at The Grammies,
you and me,
completely, entirely
in our entirety,
you and me and us.
Things that don't make sense anymore.
Things that don't make sense.

ALEX GWYTHER

Alex Gwyther has been described as *"Reminiscent of Braintax and The Streets with a wit that recalls that of Arctic Monkey's Alex Turner"*. He tells tales of life in urban Britain, such as the pound-a-pint Wetherspoon shenanigans of a Saturday night in Staines. He has performed at top festivals, venues and universities across the UK. His client list includes Help for Heroes, The Book People, Mastercard and Transitions Global. His first booklet was published by Nasty Little Press in the Spring of 2012 as part of their Nasty Little Intro's series.

AWKWARD SCENES IN A WETHERSPOON'S

We sat in an awkward silence

like an insecure couple
in a taxi ride home
after a swingers' orgy.

You sat
statue still
looking out the window sill at the grey sky,
legs crossed under the table playing with a beer mat
living off repetitive sighs

and I sat opposite

with a lion's pride
drinking London Pride
my legs wide open and stretched to one side.
I watched passersby pass us by
and pretended I was reading the drinks promotions on the
chalked up black board sign
but secretly,
I was watching you out of the corner of my eye.

We were so hungry for one another but we fasted on frowned
            expressions,
starved on stubbornness
whilst my feet foraged for a private footsy session.
We swam in silence
teased the tides of tension
and I drowned in pools of thoughts
with your mermaid figure.

Desperately ducking and dodging eye contact
I tipped the hot candle wax onto my fingertips
as sensuous-touch starved flesh bore blemishes.
We both watched as the wax welded itself onto my skin.
I peeled off the thin layer and my fingerprint was printed into the
            cream coated crater.
I flicked it towards you,
hoping you would pin prick this fingerprint
try to read in between the lines to the pattern of my thoughts,
but you just paused,
and presented me a forced and resented half hearted smile.

And that smile disappeared as quickly as light leaves a room
            when you flick the switch.
You sipped a dark silence from your Guinness and it echoed
bouncing off the walls of our tunnel vision.
Both heads bowed
but bottoms up.
And we continued this abstract telepathic conversation
debating through static airwaves
brick walled words
concave questions trapped.

We refused to give into one another.

Other couples sat cosy in candlelit corners
cradling palms, communicating in smiles,
heads tilted sharing small talk in their private cubicles.

We sat centre stage that evening.

An awkward pause lingered longer than it should've
freezing the warmth of our candlelight.

We were reduced to a spot light
and stage fright.

MY LOCAL

Saturday Night Karaoke:

The opening synths and funky guitar riff of The Bee Gees' *Night
        Fever* plays.
The local hard-nut: a shaven head British bulldog painted in
Chelsea tattoos and suffocating in gold chains is summoned up to
        the stage and takes the microphone.
His shiny black leather loafers start tapping on the tattered floor,
        his sausage fingers click to the rhythm of the song and
                his potato pelvis begins to awkwardly thrust
                        backwards and forwards.

Women sipping on fluorescent straws drag their reluctant men
        onto the intimidating dance floor –
a small space of worn carpet between the front of the bar and
        the makeshift DJ booth.

The staggering grown men hesitate at first, but are soon lured in
        by the familiar song and begin to sing along with reborn
                rhythm in their steps, roused by the British
                        bulldog now bellowing down the
                                microphone in his best high-
                                        pitched tone.

"Night Fever! Night Fever! We know how to do it!"

The mature diva's menopausal hips sway, bobbing left to right
        and the pungent smell of special occasion ladies'
                fragrance stains the taste of my pint.

Middle aged-stickframed-potbellied-bespectacled-single-men
        hold two doubles for the single ladies in the room.
The local balding John Travoltas:
silk shirts tucked into their waist high trousers, unbuttoned to the
        chest,
dazzling with shining medallions hung around their neck
throwing outdated shapes.
Red faced
laced in sexy sweat,
still grooving with a young man's flare.
Their souls, frozen in time
beneath the cool metal surface of a 1970s golden Rolex.

Built like a waiting room,
the back alcove cradles the next generation of locals entertaining
        themselves.
Clans of white suburban Romeos
doused in their father's cologne
dominate the pool table
and fruit machines
clutching onto a jazz red snakebite, cheeky Vimto or Foster's pint.
All bought with a young labourer's cash-in-hand wage.
Peroxide blonde tipped temptresses
drown in waterfalls of WKD blue.
The legless Juliets
squeezed into tubes of fabric
bulging out from their chest
squawking slurred nonsense.
Their lips,
pinching the fresh tips of cigarettes nicked from their mothers.

The last generation of locals hang like antique ornaments
blending in with the faded checkered patterns of the cushioned
        seats,
the original bricks bearing cracks in the walls,
the disused fireplace decorated with unused tools
and the uneven beams supporting the ceiling.
They sit quietly in their regular seats
drowning in real ale and whiskey thoughts of the yesteryears.

Amongst the commotion of my local's routine Saturday night
          karaoke,
my younger brother and I perch at the bar,
caught in the middle of a timeline spanning generations of locals.

We stand still and sip our drinks
with slightly awkward
out-of-town expressions.

THE CASTLE'S CURTAIN

Sat in the corner of a pub,
scenes play out in front of me.

I watch
strangers sculpt a one night stand of friendship
moulded in the space between loneliness and companionship.
They swap stories of hardship, compare broken hearts
laughing at the tarot cards they've been dealt so far.

A gargoyle man hunches on the corner of the street.
A weather worn face erased of expression,
chest inhaling the fresh fragrance of rush hour,
exchanging the days strain with the city in whispers.

I listen to
Jack-the-Lads chat about ex-girlfriends,
subtly covering sentiment and fresh broken hearts with curse
          words,
shrugged shoulders and blankets of ale.
Changing awkward small talk to sport teams and tactics.

I watch
River Island suited yuppies yap and bark
in G&T crystal puddles.
Powdering their public school noses,
showering one another in signet ring-o'-roses.

Troubled teenage eyes hide under flat cap life lines,
finding safety in the confines of a hood.
They cower in small suspicious circles,
eager to prove manhood and worth
to their elders and Uncles.

A baby-face barmaid politely smiles her way
through a tunnel of transparent compliments
to the light at the end of an eight hour shift.
Old time Billy the Kids whip outdated sweet talk from the hip
which is brushed off her thick skin.
She gathers shine in her tip jar, clock watching 'til last orders.

I glance into a dusty mirror frame.
Second hand vanity and the echoes of disused reflections.

I see
A man passing judgement on others,
dissecting them piece by piece
thinking observations,
analysing their lives in widescreen scrutiny
in a desperate attempt to make something measure in his.

REMBRANDT CLARKE

J.R. Clarke comes from a small village in the scarred moor heart of Bronte Country. He was accused of being a poet in Bristol after attempting to spleen and create in front of people, sometimes, with a microphone. This was an awkward arrangement for both parties but everyone got through it without too much decay. He says he is strictly an amateur in all aspects of life.

ANARCHIST ANARCHIST ANARCHIST
OILDRUM OILDRUM OILDRUM
CANNABINOID CANNABINOID CANNABINOID
WHERE WERE YOU

A dull red wine room squares swirl of passed on
            conical spliff
thick bloomed smoke cloud exhaled from even
            thicker lungs.
Slow wry smile of caught anecdote plucked
            from the air,
roach like soft moss left behind from
            unintentional
kisses & the nuclei of our memories that
            move us
through stages, away from time
            transisting
down stations like a radio in bad weather
            clutched by
black fog. Each gap between frequencies
            hisses white noise
but we rest briefly & each station plays a song
            of you,
or what we will become. Jazz, Rock 'n' Roll, Drum 'n' Bass
            down-beat,
a news programme, then your favourite film from childhood
            rewound backwards.

Silence
        Silence
    Crackle
           Whisper

Mayday
           Mayday
       Can you
              Hear me?

Mayday Mayday, please, come
                  get me, but
      who can hear?
Who can see those million spiders
      that spun
a steel cobweb over your mouth?
      What escape
is there from your escape? Who can forget?
      those mirrored eyes
like CCTV Cameras watching every breath rise
      out & up
away from you, then with every blink that goes
      down & lost.
Stuttering a slow prayer out in Morse for
      salvation.
To be safe again, away from knife pivot
      cliff-edge
curled up in cotton, a dreaming foetus
      waiting for
the black fog to separate before it passes away
      into white.

FRACTURE OF WHITE LIGHTS

a void, rapturous rabbit-hole
glistening paranoia, hovering over
wonky traffic-light Bristol
empty streets, connected anxiety
& unsolved mathematical proofs

when the drizzle pours
lights up my world
I unfold memories
from hours of playful
mind expansion

sit back in hard wooden chair
listen to hollow choirs
'hallelujah on the off-beat'

aching bones uncracking
like light-bulbs popping
on broken down Ferris wheel

that still turns
dull locomotion

cracking & squeaking
an endless motion

not letting the passengers off

& light-bulbs
periodically

popping
disappearing
   long
     into the night

IMITATION ISN'T FLATTERY. IT'S JUST A HOLE IN YOUR OWN HEAD

Allen Ginsberg called me up the other day.
He said I had his sunflower. "Allen,
I ain't got your flower, pal." I said "Stop fucking around kid,
I know you got it & I want it back." he said.
I thought, Shitsticks, he's onto me. But
I'm gonna bluff this out. Plus who will notice?
Who can tell the difference? A sunflower
is just a sunflower, how would anyone know?
"Allen, man, I ain't got your flower & I'd appreciate it
if you didn't call here anymore." I hung up the phone.
I mean, how could I give it back after all those hours
where we hugged & kissed the Union Jack under bedsheets
the Union Jack that coughs all night & won't let me sleep.
Twenty minutes later there was a knock on my door
I opened it. The doorframe was full
of a ten foot black suede shoe. I craned my neck out & saw
A 120 foot high Allen Ginsberg, giant in my eye.
"Hey you kid, What are you doing? Who the fuck do you think
you are? I want my sunflower back, I'm serious."
The game was up, my fraud exposed, I went back inside to get it,
the sunflower trembled in my hand as I passed it,
he grabbed it & stuck it to his side like a sceptre,
then he looked down & picked me up by the scruff of the neck,
lifting to his face. He began to speak, the air of his voice
flowed like a engine's song, cadence took me from grasp
& released me as pollen onto my own void of breeze.
"Go find your own damn sunflower." he said.

TSHAKA CAMPBELL

Tshaka was one of the 100 monkeys (#37) and does poetry to help speed up the process. It was said that he spit up Ethiopia while getting drunk with Thoth and once he read in a tabloid, that he and Crispus Attucks took the Underground Railroad to a house party in the Bronx and free-styled the Genesis story with Jesus and his Disciples. In his own words: "I have come to the realisation that I am simply a vehicle for these words; a vessel to remind us of journeys forgotten eons ago. My hope is that my work will be a reflection of the Emerald Tablet, in that every time it is read or heard, something new is extracted from its pages and vibrations."

RED DIRT

She's a
portrait of
legs long
like canoes
slicing through the crowd
neck perched
on the horizon
stretched to the ceiling
neon eyes
giraffe swallow
red
flush
lips painted blood apple
flower smile

Ethiopia earthling
eating sun
with Fingers
like flutes
why do you hide your face

behind the lies
behind the billboards
that peddle paranoia
why did you let
the metal train
scar your cheeks
'til rouge becomes flesh
'til your once fire eyes
are petrified fossils
gatekeepers of
a once born lifetime

This plantation journey
will turn your feet green
it will bend you
into seven
'til you lean
post-mortem

Your frame so slight
will be ridden
like a
drunken compass
captured by ghosts
with manicured claws
and shrapnel eyes
you will soon see
this place is death
to those willing to be fed by lions

Do not be fooled
the red dirt beneath
your fingernails
holds the genetic code to life

You will always be richer
than their propaganda

FUKUSHIMA

When you decided to falsify your safety records,
did your great great grandfather
not heavy your conscience into submission?
Didn't the mutated hands of your granddaughter's children
not clasp your fingers in defiance of their actions?
Was the sweet smell of profit
greater than that of your genetics?

Is it because your lineage never carried an aroma so perfumed
so stricken with the thick sweet nectar of acquired wealth,
your family name not as supple
as your ostrich skin lined bill fold
and the 13th zero in your bank balance?

Where will the very people you serviced
leave their remains when their peeled skin clogs drains?
How easy your name will bond with radioactive rain.

Should they drink this uninsurable catastrophe into their souls as
        penance?

Sometimes when we are earless,
and greed supersedes our humanity,
mother nature will always find a way to hold us accountable.

JAZZ

Ever
ride a woman
like a jazz riff?
Sashaying
between
notes
fingertips
barely holding on
to ends of strings
'til your body

is lifted by
and
slid
into
another
pulsing position

Snare drum
skipping across
the conversation
like dragon flies
on lily pads
chasing a New Orleans
swamp breeze
like
the bass and
piano discussing
the rigor
it takes to
dirty sex
the vocals
someone
left
laying naked
stretched and pulled
on sheet music
rocking purple
6 inch
stilettos
it's like that
as she
consumes me

Ever
press your
spirt
so far into
a woman 'til
you change

how you
both were
to be
reincarnated
next life
Your fortunes
split into
different
equators
'til her
pelvic
bone touches
China
before
reacquainting
with your
poised thrust
trembling
like
a nervous
hummingbird
as
though
you're part
of a symphony
that feels
like being acquitted
for a crime
you know you
were committing
in each swap
of surrender

I still look
over my shoulders
when I walk with her
at night
like
at any

moment
Eros himself
will
plunge through
my chest
to repossess my
heart

He would say
"Mere mortals
should not love like that.
This is meant for gods"
... as he misted back into the heavens
staining clouds
with my blood cry trailing behind him
and I would whisper to her
"don't worry baby
you are the one carrying
my heart
I didn't need
the one I held
the moment
we met"

See
in a single blink
she was burned
into my future
like the 2 sec
still image
after
a wide open
camera flash
the x-ray moment
when you're blinded

to all but
that single vision
this is how

I shape the
love I have
with her
every 2 sec
flash
a moment of
jazz scatting
her song
and
she's managed
to tool
my edges
into a gentle
riff
and a bass line
so low and
deep
it's
envied by
gods

LOVE

There's no science
in love
no periodic table
with numbers
and
abbreviated
letters
Just
two vowels
playing leap frog
in a nest
of daffodils.

SLINKY ESPADRILLES
By ASH DICKINSON

Honed over a decade of live shows, this collection could have been titled "Ash Dickinson's Greatest Hits". Featuring poems about the fear of poetry, the state of premiership football, an embalmed wife/coffee table hybrid, pollution of the oceans, a love-sick fridge and knitwear for Gibbons, it is a collection that is weird, wonderful and unpretentious.

"A very cool combination of rap, rhyme, repetition and wry wit... not only an incredibly gifted poet, but also a great comedian with a sharp eye for social commentary"
Winnipeg Free Press

ISBN 9781909136007 £7.99

THE SUSTAINABLE NIHILIST'S HANDBOOK
By JONNY FLUFFYPUNK

Achieving a state of Sustainable Nihilism has not been easy for Jonny Fluffypunk. The Genesis of this Revolutionary has involved an up-bringing of scientific exactness, complemented by experimental cross-dressing, existential fist-fights and being possessed by the spirit of a relentlessly swearing 17th Century Ranter. Nourished by fermented mysticism and the Devil's Music, Jonny takes us along for the ride as he searches for the best poem in the world.

"Whether choosing the correct towel, wearing his Mother's underwear, or reciting an ode to a dead trout, Jonny does it with a sublime mix of grace, verve, clean green jittery wit and a touch of punk rock pizzazz. The man is a genius!"
Dan Cockrill, Bang Said The Gun
ISBN 9781909136021 £7.99

Sweat-borne Secrets
By Sally Jenkinson

This is poetry from the messy world of real life, where going through the mill and the mire 'Stellared, smoking, sinning, choking', is all part of the party. Sally has an exceptional ability to capture a moment not only as a well crafted image but as an adept evocation of the emotion we feel in our hearts and stomachs.

"'Holding out a heart like a six-ounce sirloin' comes Sally Jenkinson with her poems of love and not-love. Here are urban adventures with gasmen and barmaids and Simon Armitage. Sally writes with an eye to the truth, an ear to the sound of a line and always a fierce determination to tell her truth. A strong new voice, gutsy and intelligent, worth the reading."
Jo Bell

ISBN 9781909136014 £5.99

This Is A Poem b/w A Violation Of Expectation
By Mairi Campbell Jack

In this unique double pamphlet Scottish poet Mairi Campbell-Jack applies the analytical prism of the poet's lens to two experiences that will be familiar to thousands of women: her battle to overcome post-natal depression and the break down of her marriage. The result is an eloquent examination of the intensely personal by a poet not afraid to use the bitter twists of her life as the basis for experimentation.

"This is different poetry, poetry about pain, specific, and very effective. It is also loving. What's more, the language is stunning."
Sally Evans

ISBN 9781909136052 £6.99

Shapes And Disfigurements
Of Raymond Antrobus

This third book in the Burning Eye pamphlet series presents
Raymond Antrobus, a poet from Hackney with a talent for
plucking poetry from the mouths of ordinary people. Whether a
strawberry seller in Sweden, a homeless man on a London street
or a taxi driver in South Africa, Raymond channels their voices
through his own. This is the work of a confident young poet with
an exceptional ear for language.

*"…all you need / are the right words," writes Raymond Antrobus, but
as this all-too-brief collection, demonstrates, the best poets need also
compassion, insight, craft, taste, and a pitch-perfect ear to the
cadence and tones of the human voice and mind. Antrobus has these
gifts in buckets. His monologues are stunning studies of voice and
substance, and his lyric poems are graceful and finely crafted.
Yes, he is a poet to watch, for sure.
Kwame Dawes*

ISBN 9781909136076 £5.99